THE
SHELF LIFE
of
ASHES

THE
SHELF LIFE
of
ASHES

A Memoir

HOLLIS GIAMMATTEO

[swp]

SHE WRITES PRESS

Some names and identifying characteristics have been changed to protect the privacy of certain individuals.

Published 2016
Printed in the United States of America
ISBN: 978-1-63152-047-1
Library of Congress Control Number: 2015954804

Book design by Stacey Aaronson

For information, address:
She Writes Press
1563 Solano Ave #546
Berkeley, CA 94707

She Writes Press is a division of SparkPoint Studio, LLC.

Confess your hidden faults.
Approach what you find repulsive.
Help those you think you cannot help.
Anything you are attached to, let it go.
Go to places that scare you.

From the epigraph to
The Places That Scare You, Pema Chodron

For my dearest friend, now wife, Dana Blue

CONTENTS

INTRODUCTION

⇌

A Complicated Journey

I BEGAN A MEMOIR WHEN I WAS NEWLY FIFTY, MEANING to freeze the year, to locate it as an event, an exact sensation, an experience, an obelisk that split the clouds. By the time it was "done," that year had grown into many and fifty had revealed itself to be no more identifiable than something seen teasingly far out in the ocean—is it a seal, a kelp, a piece of driftwood? Fifty compelled me to question the notion of the self,—*my* Self, an entity I had fabricated from conditions and reactions to conditions, from hopes and fears—and face certain nasty truths: that youth and all its gay attendants flee; that impermanence is king; that death will issue me an invitation with my monogram.

I submitted this memoir to myriad prospective agents and publishing houses, from which it garnered myriad rejections over a period of two years. I remember one particularly vexing "reason" I was given: "the market is glutted with books about aging; therefore, there is no market for this subject." There really is no such thing as too many books about aging, or dying, or redemption. That's like being turned away from a potluck dinner because you've brought brownies and there is already pie, three cakes, and a melon. I wasn't convinced that this was the real reason; rather, I thought it had something to do with the truth that I had not gone deeply or sincerely enough into my subject, which after all, is everybody's subject.

I put the memoir aside. I left my writing the way one leaves a bar—maudlin, reeling. I was tired of my mind, unsatisfied by the elusive nature of its products. I started gardening, began a business in that field, thinking that finally I could make things of physical beauty, employing simple values of design, making order out of nature's rich messes. But I began to wonder if, in returning to the memoir with the intention of developing my themes by bringing a more seasoned perspective to this process, I could make a parallel narrative. For my evolving sensibility—indeed, my aging—had invited my perception of this material to change. And so I decided to let the original chapters stand, following them with a commentary, adding auxiliary *and* autonomous chapters.

The original work had a problem with "inside." It neither got *inside* the experience of others' aging nor into a deeper understanding of the phenomenon itself; thus, I didn't let my reader inside me. I defended myself—my thoughts and more genuine feelings—with humor and hyperbole. In a writing project dedicated to truthful exploration, these are disingenuous ploys. I had nothing to lose by returning, I thought, and perhaps everything to gain.

Here is how I saw it *then*.

ONE

⇌

The Map of Aging Well

THE APPROACH OF MY FIFTIETH BIRTHDAY INVITED queasy speculation. Was it a beginning? An ending? A bit of both? I did not actually *feel* myself *turn* fifty, nor become, in an eye-blink, middle-aged. But I wondered, could one train for the onset of aging the way one must for a two-month bicycle trip up the Canadian Rockies, say, or any such gravely rigorous, life-altering event? I wondered could a map be found to help one through the tasks of aging? Where lay the key to, if not graceful aging, then the cultivation of a brave and resilient mind that would find something more in the process than losses heaped on losses, middens and mounds?

If I went at it as a project or a seminar, it might be possible to make an intentional transition. Perhaps by working with the elderly, I would get it in my bones and heart and tissue that I, too, was headed there. And so, on the morning of my first week after turning fifty, I sat in the offices of the Columbia Lutheran Ministries, about to have a job interview with a Jewish woman from New York City, who was a former social activist, and, I'd soon learn, dressed like me, which is to say she utilized a palette dominated by black.

Before interviewing me for a $7-per-hour job assisting a population of very old people who wanted fiercely to remain in their homes for as long as they could before being hauled out to assisted-living facilities, Harriet handed me a stack of Xeroxed forms. I looked them over. Now, I really don't mind paperwork of this nature. Filling out forms makes me feel tidy and orderly, and as if my education has accrued to something —the ability to fill out forms, for example. Where it falls apart for me is the job history. I do not *have* a job history. So whenever I apply for a job, which admittedly is not that often, and have to produce a history, I must improvise. For one thing, my jobs bear no relationship to one another. Quite the contrary. At one particularly misguided moment in my life, for example, I was going to chemical dependency counselor school. When I came to my senses and dropped out of the program, I immediately got work at the local winery. Irony has always been my guiding light in the world of work.

Even though Harriet was encouraging and the job wasn't a job so much as *research* toward discovering the Map of Aging Well, I began to sweat. I wondered, should I list my actual jobs, in which case there loomed many chronological gaps, or should I disclose that I am usually busy being a writer, which carries with it gobs and gobs of gaps in the income department? Fortunately, I had brought along my writer's résumé as an antidote to my undistinguished list of unrelated jobs.

Harriet looked at it for a long time. She looked at it and looked at it and looked at me. "Why in the world do you want to work *here*?" she asked, and this is the moment in the job interview that always stumps me, because I know that my answer will come out sounding as if I've just read an article in some dumb personal-growth magazine.

I said something about turning fifty. I said something like working with old people would teach me how to walk fearlessly through my remaining days. It was my attempt to bring aging up close to my little, squinty eyes, I said, and read its message clearly. I said something about the sad fact of my aging parents, in their eighties and so far away in Pennsylvania, and that my wanting to work with old people had the flavor of proxy about it. That is, I couldn't help my parents as they aged, but I could bear in mind their experience as I cared for others.

"With a résumé like this?" Harriet said, her eyebrows arching, her hands urging me on. Apparently, the sharing had not impressed her.

I was flattered, though, that here was someone who was actually impressed that in 1970-something I had gotten published in the *American Poetry Review*, and that my previous memoir chronicling my adventures on an all-women cross-country peace walk—though it had never as a whole seen print —had appeared in a handful of literary magazines. I was glad that I had chosen to wear black, the cuffs of my linen jacket turned halfway up my arms and my pants, though baggy, pressed. It was clearly going to be okay to be odd with Harriet.

"I'll tell you one thing," she said. "If you work for me, you'll never lack for material." That cinched it.

⇌

THAT SAME YEAR BROUGHT THE LONG PRODUCTION OF my mother's dying, as if coordinating with my quest. Oh, she'd been at it for years. But her two passions, Christian Science and hypochondria, held her in a fist of contradictory yearnings. And so she'd started calling me for help, several times a week, from where she and the Father lived in Bethlehem, Pennsylvania.

The phone would ring; I'd pick it up and hear, "Sweetie, sweetie, it's Mom," as if the two of us had been reaching out for each other, arms and hands all fluttery with love, over the Berlin Wall.

I would ask her, "How are you feeling, Mom?" This would be followed by a long pause. I'd begin to think it was my task to fill it. Mentally, I'd begin to list options: I could tell her how she was feeling; I could remind her that it was *she* who'd called; I could tell her how *I* was feeling.

Finally, she'd emerge from the pause. "I don't know," she'd say. "Robert [that was the Father] Robert, how am I feeling?" And he actually had an answer. He did not find it odd that he knew how his wife felt more clearly than she did.

I'd try to keep the ball rolling and ask, for example, for the details of her illness: its course, the types and doses of her medication. "Are you feeling better?" I'd ask. "Are you feeling worse?"

Her baffled reply suggested that the three of us should ponder this together. "I don't know," she'd cry. I could almost hear her blinking. It was really as if someone else Up There were pulling her strings.

I'd try again. "How are you feeling, Mom?"

"Well, sweetie, I'm not too tired today," she'd venture. "My goodness, I'm not tired! Where did tired go? Robert, why aren't I tired?" And from a way-back-of-the-room sort of place, I'd hear the Father's calm and patient voice: "Oxygen, dear. You are on oxygen."

"Yes, oxygen," she'd say, as if it were an item on a menu in a foreign language.

This, a representative conversation, was conducted with few changes during Mother's final year. Nothing shifted but the props—oxygen and its wicked tubing; potties; medical personnel. I thus began to anticipate the gifts of intimacy I imagined to be the landmarks of dying. I forgot, though, that intimacy had not occurred between us since we'd sat side by side on the steps of a veranda in our bathing suits, in Ocean City, New Jersey, tanned and salt-rimmed from the beach, gazing lovingly into each other's eyes. I was five. Thus, I found her current imprecations puzzling and bizarre. What comfort could I, in my present guise, bring her?

And then there was Mother's Christian Science, a knotty and all-pervasive thing. People think of Christian Science as the "you don't believe in doctors" religion, or as the religion housed in elegant, Palladian-like churches that don't look like churches, with signs above the portals saying FIRST CHURCH OF CHRIST [COMMA] SCIENTIST. Probably you've walked by these churches that do not look like churches, or past the warm, lair-like Christian Science Reading Rooms, and barely wondered. After all, ours is a culture in which whim transmogrifies to institution almost overnight and we might turn a blind eye, bent on self-protection, to the sheer volume of eccentricity parading as Truth. But pick up Mary Baker Eddy's *Science and Health with Key to the Scriptures* and open it to any page, and you will start, very quickly, to blink and feel those wrinkles deepen in your brain, the ones that signal rough seas ahead in the cognition department. You will wonder, how did this woman—a celebrity in her time, who offered a hash of half-baked Emersonian ideals and verbiage swirling in the empyrean of Lofty Language, who acquired estates and jewelry and wealth—manage all that material manifestation while stoutly denying the material world, let alone profess to hold the Key?

Equally amazing was how Mother's hypochondria, allergies, and chronic illness all huddled under the umbrella of Christian Science. Or how she understood her disease in the adherence to a faith that, despite evidence to the contrary, denied the sovereignty of the human body. No wonder the poor thing turned to her husband when asked, "How are you?" She was relieved that someone had an answer. Clearly, the Conversation of our Eternal Present signified that Mother's brain had short-circuited, what with all the contradictions.

Have I mentioned being adopted? I was. I am. I have failed horribly ever to get over it. It is and has been my defining moment, even as I lingered on my initiatory rung of middle age. There it spat and fumed, my looming, ineradicable, inerasable detail. In our frayed little familial unit, adoption remained forever our bête noire. By virtue of their cool unwillingness to ponder, to entertain, to breathe in the complex bouquet of our fabricated family, my relationship with the Parents pickled in the brine of disappointment. I, too, disappointed, exhausting them with my endless curiosity and questions, forever pounding my issues like meat, forever working to solve "the adoption problem," as if I were masticating gristle. Their silence was impressive, a natural force—the San Andreas Fault of lost opportunity.

Thus, we drifted. Continental drift characterized my

relationship with my adoptive parents. So when Mother began to importune four decades later, "Sweetie, I'm scared. Come home," imagine my surprise at being reined back into the family circle. In the last year of Mother's life, to be cast in the role of "loving daughter" would prove, I reasoned, either a text written by the absurdists or a chance to find some mercy and to mend.

But my dread at going "home" proved an obstacle. It had taken grit and ingenuity to flee west, to plant my feet on the ground when I stopped running, and to learn to trust the solidity of feet and ground, what with all that lofty, concept-burdened Christian Science. In saying yes to Mother and experiencing the complications of my choice, I would, of course, have to write about it—the tedium, the guilty irritation, the queasy fears, the ill will and resentment, the moment or two of grace.

It was like a flight to Europe: You board the plane. It is one of those wide, wide planes with five seats on either side and about an acre of seats in the middle. It is a veritable football field of a plane. Everyone climbs onboard with tidy bundles, looking crisp and eager. A solid hope prevails—in efficiency, good cheer, the sustained excitement in the going, and, most of all, the arrival without mishap. Shoes are shiny, reading matter at the ready, bottled water tucked under every arm. The plane takes off. Everything is working—the toilets, the flight attendants, the terrible forced air. Blankets, folded neatly in sterile plastic wrapping, support the anticipation of happy sleep.

And then, midflight, it starts to fall apart. Everybody's hair has flat spots. Everybody's clothes are wrinkled. Eyes are rimmed with sleep; everyone has a crooked, puffy face. The toilets have not flushed since the mid-Atlantic. Toilet paper ran out somewhere over Greenwich. The aisles look like a dirty river. Debris and garbage bob. Four hours into the flight, the plane seems to have run out of air and everyone has been inhaling everyone else's racking coughs and wet sneezing. Backs seize up. Legs will not unbend. The illusion of crisp efficiency in the little world of the Boeing has been shattered.

My experience of Mother's dying is that flight. Writing about it gives you and me the illusion that there was a clean narrative line, that the event—even that there was an *event*—produced insight, action, dramatic changes in behavior, and on and on. In the end, it has more accurately been the jet a few hours out of Newark, caught between the excitement of *here we go* and the exhausted flight attendants maintaining cheer in the face of the toilets overflowing.

⇌

Commentary:

CONTRADICTIONS

IN THE ORIGINAL MEMOIR, I ONLY HINTED THAT MY quest was shaped by a spiritual perspective, one quite emphatically the opposite of Christian Science. I hoped that the tone employed in setting a scene, or the way I described myself in that scene, would signal "spiritual perspective" to my readers. I asked you to trust my authority without revealing my "credentials." Buddhist practice has been my moral rudder and my lens through which to view myself for over thirty years, and, unlike Christian Science, constantly urges compassionate engagement. Revisiting this memoir invited me to make explicit connections between my encounters with the elderly and Mother and the dharmic principles so rich and useful in a life: impermanence, emptiness, no self, the Five Precepts, the Four Noble Truths, mainly. The memoir, after all, is my tale from brokenness to integration, from despair to a kind of atonement, and one doesn't board that train without required reading, nutritious snacks, and sturdy luggage.

In the commentaries, I hope to add depth through maturity —the power of spiritual practice; the theme of loss that dogs so many of our actions and all of our days; the impact of growing up in Christian Science; issues of identity that can accompany the experience of being adopted.

Christian Science, for example, a source of mockery in the original, turned into the desire to understand how its skewed philosophy informed my relationship with Mother and how I might come to identify its grip. I hoped that learning something of its history and the context that enabled its trajectory would let me come to see it as yet another example of history's rich jokes and unjust terrors, and so end my persecution.

The original memoir offered a beginner's thoughts and observations on aging. For this, I enlisted characters in my work as a companion for a Lutheran organization called Club 24, which invariably would slip out as "Cloud 9." Cloud 9 it wasn't. My aged characters struggled, and out of their suffering, conscious or otherwise, I wrung vignettes. I didn't empathize so much as project upon them. I hope in the commentaries to be kinder and make a fuller story.

And the memoir is concerned with identity—its more customary falseness, arbitrary nature, and fragility. Adoption makes identity a living question—for parents and children alike, I think. Of course, we are all the playthings of chance. But in the absence of the grounding omphalos of the biological family, adoption throws, quite early on, an existential wrench. Identity is a freedom and a shackle; it creates itself, shifts, and moves away like a cat descending a flight of stairs. Above the stairs and treetops, the morning sky is brilliant, and the cat, with no apparent shift in position, melts into its own long, downward reach from stair to stair. Sunlight passes over its back as it continues its slow, dappled way down. The sun freckles the cat's back like fish darting between rocks. And then it's gone. One moment, the more-or-less-solid movement of the dappled cat, the next, merely light and shadow. It hasn't leapt. It is not hiding in the bushes; rather, it's dissolved, as if becoming the movement of its own cells and breathing. Has it possibly slipped into an invisible pocket of something to be carried along that current and to reappear a solid cat, reassembled on the concrete curb? But nothing. It has shifted into dappled air.

That is how our fragile hold on identity still strikes me.

T W O

⇌

A Medley of Awkward Changes
and Flagging Self-Esteem

AT THE TIME OF MY EMPLOYMENT WITH CLUB 24 AND
Mother's long demise, I was living in Belltown, a Seattle
neighborhood characterized chiefly, as my own life had so far
been, by sheer *potential*. For decades, Belltown enjoyed a
reputation of dank seediness and squalor. Compensatory
institutions, such as the Catholic Seamen's Club, soup kitchens
and flophouses scattered hither and yon, and an infamous
watering hole named My Suzi's, served a population of sailors,
old and young, and those odoriferously, chronically down on
their luck. The oxymoronic Labor Temple presided over a city
block between Cedar and Broad.

Over time, Belltown upgraded and the derelict influence
expanded to welcome drug addicts, the certifiably insane, and
artists. However sad or sinister this part of town, it retained
vista-rich expanses where one could stroll amid debris and
beggars, breathing in the good, salty air, able to look,
unimpeded, across the moody bay to the snowy peaks of the

Olympics. And then, suddenly, Belltown caught the eye of developers, and so began an orgy of construction.

First to go was the vacant lot beside my small apartment building. It was not an inspiring piece of ground—in the middle of downtown, how could it be—a catchall for mendicant plastic bags and paper scraps. Dog poop lined the cyclone fencing like dull but fragrant garnish. Fennel grew and flourished and in the heat of summer afternoons offset the smell of poop with a licorice fragrance, heady and brave. There were great jolts of grass and the yellow tassels of the fennel, and at least one tenant would be walking a dog in the little tract whenever I passed. Although it was not a terribly pretty place, that it was an open tract sporting all that fennel and affording the absence of urban frenzy so that a dog could have a stretch and the eye could roam, wasn't that worth something? Naturally not. Within a year would come convoys of great machinery and troops of men in hard hats and lunch pails, and of course there went the days of easy parking. Construction began. The perfecting of a hole that would in turn provide the parking pit and the foundation for the luxury condo high-rise took one whole year. My beleaguered fellow tenants and I were launched from sleep at six thirty every morning by noises typically associated with modern warfare.

Internal forces mustered. The body, too, began to toot the torments of menopause. No longer an intriguing mirage glimpsed in the distance, it had come upon me. Nothing less than An Event of the Body, it sang its truth that the body will have its way. The discomforts imposed mimicked such nonfatal torments as hangover, chills and fever, ennui and dread. I'd leave home, turn the corner, and walk right into a hot flash. My dazzling and disorienting menopausal symptoms

—which, like adolescence, brought the knowledge that however earnest and industrious our minds, the body's truth is sovereign—were offset by the thrill of knowing that any moment I'd stop pouring a fortune into the feminine-hygiene industry. The fifties and adolescence indeed felt similar, except my decade lacked the thrill of naïveté and illusion. Both in adolescence and in old age, the future looms. But the former floats a kind of hopefulness over a landscape of primary colors and views unobstructed by the neighbor's, for example, augmentation of her roofline, while the latter is a land where gray predominates and all you can think of, bitterly, is your stolen view.

Further incidents: my eyes now saw as if through a smudged and dirty windowpane. There had been no distance as yet invented to accommodate this kind of vision. Faces blurred. I couldn't hold comfortable conversations. While I sat across from lover or friend, with glasses on, the face leaped into a crisply rendered landscape filled with pores and pimples, streaks of errant makeup, an eyelash tumbled onto a pitted cheek. I preferred to view my friends sans specs, as the more familiar and lovable blots and blurs.

There was the awkwardness of morning aches; the stiffness of hands exposed a tad too long to cold. There was the fear that my sex life would expire in what might begin as a small plea—"I'd rather watch telly tonight, dear. How about you?"—and extend into a guilty, dry forever. There were distressing terms, like "dry vagina," that women of my age would read and then think, with a shudder, *I am living on borrowed time.*

No doubt about it, my flesh was losing bounce. To reconcile, I started reading about the practice of Buddhist monks in ancient times, who, by sitting in the charnel grounds to meditate on corpses in various stages of decay, hoped to bring death into a day-to-day awareness. Where, I wondered, was today's analogy? Where could one go for such pungent reminders of the self's departure? The neighborhood alley onto which backed several fast-food restaurants, each with several teeming Dumpsters all its own, was about it. There on a hot summer day, for example, one might sit on the lip of a Dumpster and ponder the natural phenomenon of decay while smelling imploding melons; crow-pecked, greasy bones; soggy pizza leavings, the blood-rot smell of old meat; perhaps a little throw-up; the raw, rambunctious waft of fortified wine from an almost-empty bottle. Dignity does not derive from Dumpster study, of course, but seriously, I ask you, where else in Belltown can you go?

One afternoon, I was hoisting my bike onto the car's rooftop rack. That I could do this at all satisfied me deeply, implying as it did that I was not yet decrepit and decayed. I'd just completed an hour-long ride, which included more uphill terrain than down. A friendly man, passing me on foot, noticed both my hoisting and the virtuous glow of my exertion. "How many miles?" he asked me.

I answered, "Oh, no more than eight miles. Down to the lake and all the way back up." I shrugged to emphasize that he needn't be impressed on my behalf.

"Honey," he said, "I know people *half* your age who can't even walk a block without huffing."

That stopped my mind. Not how you might think. The compliment proved that the signs had grown obvious; others had begun to view me differently from how I viewed myself. I did not like having this brought to my attention.

I do not *feel* like the sort of person who is older than "people half my age." I feel like those people who *are* half my age, meaning I believe that I look like them, and the truth is, according to this kind, supportive passerby (incidentally, I couldn't tell how old *he* was), I do not look like the people whose ages I think I look like. There are the places along the jawline where the skin has begun to pull away, the flesh of thigh that has transformed from its accustomed tautness of burnished skin to what is called, appallingly, "crepe."

I wish I were the sort of person who could just relax. Just take it easy. Survey the human condition for what it is—a logistical nightmare that involves a lot of shlepping—and kick back, keep the cooler filled with refreshing beverages, and do what needs doing. Make money. Reproduce. Attend funerals and weddings. Learn to like parades. Proudly acquire such collectibles as Bakelite, rotary telephones, antique weather vanes, or Tupperware containers. But no. I had to turn fifty over and over again, until my resistance to it stiffened, like a fallen leaf, and the breeze bore it away.

Why did I contend that fifty, this marker of a life half done, was a phase to be entered with alacrity, grace, and perspective? I had succumbed to the belief that the decades heralded pertinent tasks to be mastered. This suggested a rehearsal frame of mind. I would rehearse being fifty, as one, in childhood, rehearsed bicycling with the help of training wheels. I would wobble, career, and fall, but, by God, I would master *middle age.*

I let my actual birthday go by, spending it in a fidget, ignoring imprecations from friends to celebrate hugely. I avoided it intensely. One year later, when I turned fifty-one, I had a fiftieth birthday party for myself. I "themed" it, intending it to be an opportunity to celebrate impermanence, and invited those who had a high tolerance for my spiritual shenanigans. Every year, I would try turning fifty again, entering the decade as if it were an enchanted wood.

All I really wanted to do was talk about this with some sympathetic soul, and where better to turn over such morbid thoughts than with those who can contain the miseries of the flesh, its horrors? It occurred to me that this hunger to share would be perfectly served if I worked in a morgue.

What would I do there, you wonder? I thought of myself as a greeter. I would pet the bodies and welcome them, making sure everyone had a nametag. I would improve their hair, adding, if not luster, at least a semblance of tidiness. Eventually I would learn how to perform autopsies. Biology, after all, had been my favorite class in the seventh grade. My best friend in the seventh grade was my very own cat corpse, steeping in formaldehyde. Mrs. Scibo was my very favorite teacher, along with Ms. Oliver, who taught zoology and looked like a Don Martin cartoon out of *MAD* magazine and was known to store her lunch in the lab refrigerator reserved for the dissected remains. Oh, how I loved to learn the miraculous, inner workings of our small cadavers, and the special challenge of recognizing the actual body part after studying those textbook illustrations that gave one the idea that the innards lay in tidy stacks and layers, all primly outlined and color-coded and helpful with arrows and labels.

Because I am the sort of person who can never just relax, who when seized by an idea am not content merely to let it picnic in my little brain patch and then float merrily away, I buy a lot of books to hoist my questions toward Significance and then make many phone calls to Experts in the Field. In this case, I tracked down such people as the county coroner, the police, the morgue folks, and anyone whom I thought might know how I could engineer my career change from, well, nothing in particular, with some well-developed language skills (that would be my English-major background), to An Autopsy Person.

Appalled, my friends asked, "Why?"

I replied, "I like dead people."

The truth was, I'd never known a dead person. Oh, yes, I knew people who had died, but I didn't know them as, you know, *dead people.* Mother, ill for years, had begun to worsen. Her diagnosis was a rare—of course it would be *rare*—a chronic pulmonary disease called mycobacterium avium. So with that, I reasoned, soon I'd know one. Naturally, the horrible and guilt-inducing thought followed: Would I prefer my mother as a dead person to a living one? Once Mother was dead, after all, the possibility of memories uncensored by such challenges to relationship as narcissism and situational hearing loss loomed unfettered. Nostalgia might bloom. I might actually miss her. Not that I expected communication from her once she passed. Since her worldly advice ran a modest gamut from ironing tips to the crucial significance of vitamin supplements, I figured that her contribution would not be much regarding news from the other world, or the beyond, or the afterlife, or whatever it is we lapsed Christians are wont to call it.

BUT BEFORE I COULD PUT INTO ACTION MY PLAN OF working in the morgue, I spotted Harriet's ad, and so I had to tuck the idea back into the cabinet of future dreams.

My first potential model for graceful aging was Pauly Amos. Harriet described my job with her as simple—"Making order," she said, adding coyly, "things are never what they seem."

Pauly's son had moved her to a roomy Queen Anne apartment, in which she had dwelt, unpacked, for the last two years.

My first Pauly Amos morning, I was greeted by a tiny, dreadful dog named Chad. A Yorkshire Terrier, Chad was the sort of mammal that looks like a cleaning implement. He liked me at once. He demonstrated his affection by licking every part of my leg from the moment I got there until leaving time. Being old, Chad had teeth that fell out willy-nilly. I would find them here and there—on the sofa, on a chair, underfoot— curdled brown nuggets that amended the content of Pauly's carpet with organic content.

I realized from the moment of meeting Pauly that our relationship would be contentious. About the reason for my employment, we disagreed. *She* thought it was to share a little reminiscing and to leisurely go through the two years' accumulation of junk mail. *I* thought it was to unpack her and make at least some walkways through, over, and around her stuff. It did not take social-worker perspicacity to note that in the garbage bags full of do-not-ask, the dirty dishes and glasses in do-not-ask sorts of places, the undiscarded, empty tins of dog food, and the omnipresent heaps of mail, a little mental illness was afoot.

Now Discard is my middle name. I live to toss and tidy. Lead me to a shifting pile of magazines and curly-edged papers, and I'll give them three seconds to shape up, or out they go. Belts? Unmated socks? Heirlooms that look like tchotchkes? Rusty garden tools? Pot metal flatware? I am the Great Leveler when it comes to *stuff*.

The first task that Pauly set us to was sorting through the mail. The problem was that we'd no sooner start than she'd get really, *really* engaged with what came to hand—*last* spring's

Nordstrom catalog, for example, or next spring's glossy brochure for some impossibly expensive cruise to Malta. Back they'd go onto her "save" pile. So I tricked her. I urged her, for example, to read all of the fine print in the brochures, and then, when she was good and engaged, I quickly hid my admirable discard pile under a corner of the rug. Later, I reasoned, I would walk all of it down to the Dumpster.

We lasted two weeks as an item, Pauly Amos and I. According to Harriet, the reason Pauly didn't want me was that she had a problem with my age. I was too fit, she said. Pauly couldn't quit resenting that I rode my bike to her apartment. She couldn't get over the fact that I had a working set of legs. She couldn't get over the fact of my relative youth.

With this first disappointment, my search for the Map of Aging Well only intensified. I wondered, would the ingredients prove to be one part wisdom, two parts exhaustion? When you got finished with dread, sadness, and denial, in the end, probably, you just ran out of steam, letting wisdom emerge from the vapor.

⇌

Commentary:

ANOTHER DAMN CANCER STORY

I CAN SEE NOW THAT I MADE TOO BIG A FUSS ABOUT menopause. It was a sojourn in Cancer Land that would lend perspective. I was lucky. (See how quickly my words rush in to reassure you.) I was lucky in these ways: it was detected early;

the lump was minuscule, the lymph nodes clean; my procedure was simple—two lumpectomies followed by ten weeks of radiation. I had my summer plan.

I cannot make any sense of this experience, still. My life did not feel threatened; I held that fear in check. Were I to be given a biopsy report that found cancer in my lymph nodes, then, I reasoned, I'd exhibit full-throttle hysteria. Assuredly, the diagnosis got my attention. I diverted an emotional reaction to my special news into a strategy of vigilant compliance: I would do everything they—oncologist, nurse practitioner, naturopath, radiologist—told me to do, and thus proceed quickly through it. As a recipient of cancer care, I experienced minor insults—the obsequious regard of a surgeon whose role, allegedly key, remained ambiguous. He had the longest face I've ever seen, sort of like John Kerry's stitched onto Dick Van Dyke's —handsome in an almost sort of way. He rubbed his hands together and bobbed toward me, this odd gait magnified by the smallness of the room and the lack of space between my jutting knees and the door, where he loomed. He seemed to savor his role as both the bearer of bad news and the chief comforter. The flaw in this was embedded in projection. He projected onto me the fear and dismay and bafflement and rage that he assumed to be my cancer companions. He petted my knee and gave me an unguent of assurance, speaking kindly, speaking slowly. He knew what I had to be feeling. The nurse would handle that. Pressing his tie to his heart, he retreated, vowing, "*We* are here for you."

Onto such tiny moments, I imposed the larger feelings I could not contact in my consciousness, or what seethed beneath. Similar, though less disingenuous, phenomena occurred when I shared my news with friends. My experience was up for grabs,

I learned, before I could even own it. When I mentioned my cancer, people rarely paused to let the moment of disclosure penetrate and give rise, then, to reflection, but instead immediately and intensely projected: "My God. Your whole life must have passed before your eyes!" or "I bet that helped straighten out your priorities!" Rarely was I able, in sharing, to have my own experience. So I stopped. I honestly didn't know how I felt and didn't want to be taken hostage by feelings not my own.

Cancer scaled down the comic goings-on about my menopausal ills. *Cancer* is a bigger word than *menopause*, although sadly breast cancer has become, for women in the United States, almost a rite of passage.

Does one say "*my* cancer" or "*the* cancer," unadorned? Was it mine? For all I knew, I could be cancer's minion.

My left breast sports a divot from the radiation; its tissue exhibits a variety of textures, from Styrofoam packing peanuts to charbroiled meat to freshly tanned leather. My breasts no longer occupy the same plane. My burnt breast seems to have slid down its chest wall. Their appearance doesn't bother me, nor does the divot. I'm not vain of breasts. Or I am, in the sense that life writes upon our bodies, marking us like tooled leather. I am telling this because I don't know what to make of it, while I believed I knew exactly what to make of menopause. But in the rants, I could be funny, and cancer isn't funny, by most accounts. What is funny, however, is the plethora of products "for the cure": corn starch and sneakers; key chains and soda pop; tube socks and breakfast cereal. The incongruous coupling of cure products inspires its own incongruity: gratitude and cynicism.

I received the confirmation of my diagnosis while visiting the Father. Mother had been dead for several years; that gave him reason to believe, or hope, that the two of us might grow into a Family. I didn't want to grow anything with him, but my father was ninety by then and I owed him something. The visit had been planned for a while, and a day before, on the birthday of my wife, Dana, I had been called back to mammography to have some ambiguity on my film reassessed. That led to an immediate call for an ultrasound, and, instead of meeting Dana for our dinner date, I called her from the hospital. She found me in the labyrinthine basement of Radiology, where I was jellied up and about to be scrolled over. The procedure seemed to last a long time; concern took the room temperature up a notch, and a physician was called in for consultation. He studied the screen, trying to look neutral. Dana, who had had myriad and varied experiences in hospitals and with medical staff, knew just how to ask him for *confidential* information.

"It doesn't look good," he said. "I'm concerned."

I was, in the way of these things, scheduled to deliver myself to the Father the very next morning. Dana would contact me with the news.

I WAS THERE FOR A DAY WHEN SHE CALLED TO GIVE ME the diagnosis. The Father was taking his nap.

"What should I do?" I asked her, numb, dreading this change in plans. I was afraid to disappoint him. I was afraid to share my fear.

"Come home," she said, without hesitation.

"I can't. I'm here. I can't stand to tell him."

"Tell him. Then come home."

It seemed I was more afraid of disappointing my father and the plan than I was of dying.

"When is the surgery?" I asked. It was scheduled for later the same week.

We hung up. After a great, empty pause, I woke him. I didn't want to tell him, because there had never been a moment of emotional honesty between us, at least not one that might build upon itself, evolving into trust. Emotions to my father were unpleasant glitches relegated to womankind whose tasks also included laundry, menstruation, mildew management, and childbirth. He shuffled into the living room, lowering himself in rickety stages onto the apricot-colored couch. I dispensed with prelude.

"I got a call from Dana," I said. "I've been diagnosed with breast cancer." It *sounded* so much worse than I felt it to be. It's disproportionate to have such a Big Word determine the fate of your body, which bears no signs, symptoms, or sensations. Would there come a moment when the two fused? For now, the experience was more like getting ready for a camping trip —there is the list, the procuring of gear, the maps, the vehicle serviced. As I said, I had my summer plan.

My father's eyes widened with a look of sympathy and love. That was the door, then—one honest moment. We sat quietly and talked. The afternoon slid by. He was so very sorry. We talked about old friends, deceased or suffering from dementia. Of course he would take me to the airport in the morning. I did not expect this, any of it. He had been to me, for many years, the Father—incurious, judgmental, condescending, impatient for me to rein myself in and conform.

And so from that future moment on, I couldn't call him the Father anymore. He would become Pop—as in "Hi, Pop," when I called him—or the Ancient One, when I talked about him with friends. Cancer had begun to cook us.

THREE

⇋

Helen

MY NEXT CHARGE, HELEN, WOULD BRING MORE SUCCESS, because she did not begrudge me my relative youth or my working set of legs. Harriet issued me the job description: "Just sit with her. Nod and listen. Get her to take a walk. She's got Parkinson's. She's got to move. Otherwise, do nothing."

She lived in a lovely, older house in Magnolia, a westerly hump of town, accessed by a thrilling crescent of land that rose over the port's vast acreage and railroad yards, and then across an old, two-lane bridge and up Madrona Boulevard, a wide, sweeping street along the bluffs, lined with palatial homes. In the drizzly, gusty autumn, myriad shades of gray dimpled and pearled the water in the near distance, sailboats, here and there, like sharp accents. Helen, divorced for years, lived in what are fondly, British-ly called reduced circumstances; most of those living on the bluff were regarded as rich. She occupied a constant paranoid certainty of being ripped off.

Helen reminded me of Mother. Pleasant and seemingly self-effacing, both put their trust in outside authority, like little girls. Both seemed silly in their mental dishevelment— Mother, with her "Robert, Robert, how am I?" and Helen with her useless memory aids. Festooning the top of a lampshade were little prayer flags of Post-its—phone numbers with their attending names, forgotten; to-do items accompanied neither by dates nor by other organizing details; health tips clipped from Sunday magazines; expired coupons.

Helen spent her time sitting in an upright chair in a dim corner of the living room, beside the memory lamp, Mrs. Slumped in Her Chair Against the World's Perfidy and Evil. This chair, which I always found her in, was a leather, upright, library-ish sort of chair, not designed for comfort. There she quivered and shook, pondering some horror or clutching some body part in a frozen spasm of despair. It seemed that just paying a bill or making an appointment exposed Helen to the terrible knowledge that malignant forces and vile plotting to divest her of her sanity and fortune were a blink away.

"How are you, Helen?" I asked on our first day.

"Terrible, honey. I'm just terrible today," she replied, bracing herself between the doorjamb and an ebony cane as she struggled to open the door. A tall, well-groomed woman, Helen dressed carefully, her outfits climaxing in a blond-streaked, looming wig. I reached for her arm, but she patted me away.

"You mustn't touch me today, honey," she said in a rapid, breathless little voice. "I fall down, you see."

Helen maintained that she was being ruined by Bulgarians —her housekeepers and handymen and such. Over the years, sons had arrived from Bulgaria, and sons of sons, and their original immigrant bungalow, in Helen's mind, teemed with relatives all in some way seeking jobs to inflict upon her. In her reports, her house had a way of sounding annexed.

One afternoon, I found her door cracked open and heard the drone of the television. The house was dimmer than usual. She was watching *The Bridge on the River Kwai* on a television set so old, the colors flickered between purple and pale green. A plate balanced noncommittally on her sloping lap. It held half a sandwich. She wore a leopard-print dress, soft black pumps, and stockings rolled just below the knee. The wig slouched over her brow more than usual.

"I'm a basket case today, honey." The tremor in her hand that held the sandwich scattered its filling on the floor. "I'm so tired, honey, really," she said.

"You look tired, Helen," I said. "You look pale."

"Do I, honey? Pale, too?" she asked, worried but at the same time confirmed in the belief of her own fragility.

I went into the kitchen to get her a glass of water and noticed that my feet made those sucking noises like when you're in the movie theater, trying to leave your seat, and realize you've been steadily sinking into some old puddle of spilled soda pop and whatever else—you'd rather not imagine. When I tried to lift my shoes, they made a dirty, dispirited noise. For the first time, I pried myself away from the splendor of the views out every window, and the basic graciousness of her old house, and realized that it was, in fact, filthy in spite of the alleged Bulgarian intervention. The blue linoleum of the kitchen floor bore a film, and in significant intersections, where stove met molding for example, a buildup of grease and fallen food had formed crusted drifts. My feet were telling me the depth of Helen's isolation.

"Helen, don't your Bulgarians clean your floor?" I asked.

She pondered. "Well, maybe last Sunday they mopped it," she ventured.

"My feet are sticking to the kitchen floor," I said.

"Yes, I've noticed that, honey," she agreed sweetly.

"Would you like me to mop?" I asked.

"That would be okay, honey—you go right ahead."

"What do you supposed happened out there?" I asked.

She shrugged good-humoredly. "Somebody spilled honey?" she ventured.

Letting the improbability of that pass, I searched the broom closet to pull out an ancient, withered mop and an almost-empty container of Mop & Glo. There was nothing authoritative or bold with which to aggress upon the floor.

I imagined her, standing by the sink in her gray kitchen, reaching for a grape or any food scrap that came readily to hand, gazing out over her splendid view, paralyzed by the simplest procedure of caring for herself. I imagined her unable to muster even a memory of when the floor had been washed last.

When I finished, I saw that she was still sitting limply in her chair. In the past month, her leopard-print frock could no longer conceal the food and beverage spills. A trail of grapes on the floor from the kitchen to her chair leaped into view. Earlier, she'd taken a bunch into the living room. Most would be anywhere by now. With the help of the Bulgarians, they'd remain where they'd fallen for weeks and no one would be the wiser.

BY LATE FALL, THE MADRONA TREES LOST THEIR BRAZEN color. They looked peaked, their leaves a weary yellow. My final task would be helping Helen get ready for her Thanksgiving trip to Texas, where her daughter and grandchildren lived. On this day, her paranoia landed in the fixed belief that her daughter was setting a trap, trying to lure her down to Texas in order to put her in "the home."

Her agitated trains of thought collided and derailed even more than usual. By Helen's account, her daughter—an impatient, middle-aged woman—hosted vile, self-serving intentions about her mother's fate. I thought about my mother and wondered how I fared in her accounts of my behavior. That I couldn't—or wouldn't—drop everything and "come home" surely signified my callous self-regard. The relief of exchanging Mother for Helen had been short-lived.

More or less together, we advanced upon Helen's cupboard to pack up her pills. There were five kinds each of the same pills in various colors, brands, and doses; bottles half empty, half full; pills the point of which had long ago been lost; pills Helen swore she'd die without. Two hours later, after I had sorted and packed and set a perfectly calibrated amount of pills for Texas, she forgot what we were doing and demanded that we begin again.

Next, we had to prepare and pack the extra wig. It had its own special box, which I was eager to open in order to regard a fresh new wig without all of Helen's history and oddness pressed into it. With a little thrill of revulsion mixed with worry, I opened the box. There it lay, an intricate nest—a slightly frosted, "aren't we ready for a night out on the town?" affair—that looked nothing whatsoever like the thing on Helen's head. On Helen's head routinely perched a mat that had ceased to care whether it had a night out on the town or even whether it resembled hair. Looking more like a field of flattened grass, the wig dipped across her forehead in a robust swoop. It occurred to me that she did not know that one must comb and set these things. Helen's wig functioned more like a beret.

Next came the challenge of sorting through piles and bags and shelves of junk in a room set aside for "I'll deal with this later, honey." After years of Later, Later was today. The room teemed with stuff contained and uncontained—contained in black garbage bags, brimming and unclasped, and uncontained in mounds of wadded clothes, elephantine piles of newspapers and Sunday magazines, broken chairs, and rolls of shredding carpet. The accumulation was geology, but inane and unrelated —health bulletins boasting of new illnesses and trendy cures; the stray boot; the rumpled pinafore; empty pill bottles—and all revealing a mind unable to sort or discard with the aid of reason.

Pawing idly through a pile of baby clothes, she paused, stopped by a worry of the Thanksgiving visit. "I'll just be in the way," she said. "No one wants someone who will just be in the way." The silk scarf she'd been holding, festooned with horse heads and lucky horseshoes, fluttered at her side as she started crying. I dropped thirty pounds of yellowed *Reader's Digest*s and crossed the dark room to hug her. "Oh, Helen, you're not just somebody in the way. You're wonderful and funny, and they love you," I said. "You're going to have a wonderful trip. It will be all right."

"We're on the same wavelength, honey, you and I," she said, drying her eyes. The valve of hope had opened. Her blue eyes sparkled, and the next thing I knew, she was trying to extract a promise that when—not *if*—she returned from the holiday, I would be her *special* person and come work for her every day. But I knew this was our last good-bye.

Even were she to return, the truth of it was, I couldn't keep a boundary with Helen. I was easily seduced by her hope that I'd be, indeed, her special person, an honorary, if surrogate, Bulgarian. Nor could I position myself appropriately in relation to Helen's basic needs. She was an old woman suffering from Parkinson's and some form of dementia. I was a writer suffering from the need to make meaning, or more meaning, out of this limited, contractual relationship. After all, it was the limitations that defined the job.

I loved that she was silly. Helen was Beckett crossed with Zen—a desperate condition lightened by a plunge into the present moment. One afternoon, we took a long walk. That is, it took a long time to walk around the block, given her Parkinson shuffle and the elliptical attention span. We enjoyed a Beckettian exchange, as she described her travels. "Around the world in a straight line, honey," she said. "Now, why did I do that, honey, I wonder," she added.

We stopped by a weeping Japanese maple, the color of red wine. For a long time she pondered, and then looked at me with those direct and beautiful periwinkle eyes. She seemed to think for a while longer and then fell into the contentment of gazing at the leaves underfoot, fallen from the maples like crimson stars.

"Where did you go, exactly?" I asked.

"Somewhere in a straight line, honey, all around the world. It took six weeks," she said.

Helen was, if nothing else, present moment. No grounding details, no cumbersome context—merely the process of wondering at this strange life. After I said good-bye to Helen, my experiment seemed like a piece of Absurdist Theater, not well thought out and doomed to fail. My bold intent to stare aging in the eye was sabotaged by too much distance between my *here* and Helen's *there*. Unlike Helen, I didn't know what scenarios awaited me. Even the desire to know hid, forgotten and out of reach, like the stuff you never think you'll need in the tall, barely accessible kitchen cupboard, where all of it vies for the darkest corner—the broken blender, the stash of ancient paper plates, the dog-eared party napkins, one-third bag of old cat food, those healthy snacks you continue buying that never transcend the taste and the texture of packing material. Up it all goes into the hardest-to-reach, tallest kitchen cupboard, to be dragged out only when you need the space or in an emergency.

⇌

Commentary:

THE CABINET OF CRAVING AND GREED

IT WOULD HAVE BEEN THE EASIEST THING IN THE WORLD to steal from Helen, and not necessarily out of malice and certainly not out of need, but out of raucous boredom. I was sunk in torpor. I was supposed to be helpful in practical, cheerful ways. What could have been simpler?

My conflict—the urge to Do Good and Live Simply—confronted my terror of a wasted life in the avoidance of any conflict or challenge to Goodness and Simplicity. This urge to the Good was constantly upended by the factual paralysis the job's limitations engendered. The job of companioning demands intimacy without the authority to author change. A companion may spend more time with her ancient charge than does currently a son or daughter, but the companion, queen of the quotidian, has no power to affect the charge. She must collude with delusion or deception—not always, of course. But more often than not, the ancient charge should have been moved to an assisted-living facility, while his or her delusion, and the unpleasant difficulty of challenging it, puts everyone in the mode of treading water.

I saw Helen twice a week, totaling eight hours, for five months. Why couldn't I have been content with the Good and Simple tasks that constituted helping her? Because I was bored. I had set up this project to "get" aging, and I realized that the idea was far more attractive than its execution. When I entered Helen's home, I had to quell the urge to flee. Decrepitude and unmetabolized despair undid me. Desperate to escape, I might indulge in snooping. Helen might sit in her dim corner, dozing, adrift on the contents of her mind, recalling the podiatrist, anticipating Texas, pondering the inexplicable Post-it note held between quaking fingers—did it refer to something past or something yet to come?

I propelled myself from languor with my curiosity. What did Helen's bedroom look like? What was in the basement? Were her drawers tidy or a mess? For I could know only a sliver of the Helen self through the tone of a request uttered from the corner, bits of memory laced with hurts and worry, the occasional intact anecdote, all and only known in the isolation that we shared.

One day, on a pretext, I explored the basement and discovered a cache of impressive wine—Rothschild Bordeaux, as I recall. This triggered recollections of my college drinking days, enhanced by bouts of kleptomania. A grand challenge to my dexterity had been the quantity of bottles I managed to fit inside a capacious fur coat, plucked from a thrift store and worn for these occasions. It had wide-cut arms with fitted cuffs and deep pockets. My record was six: sleeves, pockets, and waistband—fore and aft.

Upon discovering Helen's cache, I felt a wave of giddiness sweep over me. I stood before the cabinet—shoulder height; dark, splintery wood; three shelves packed with the titillating bottles—and started to scheme. I don't know how long I stood there; I wrestled for a long time with my conscience. It would, as I noted, have been the easiest thing in the world to make off with Helen's stash. She was already more or less in Texas, from which she might not even return. And then there was the question of her memory—a time-travel machine at best.

I would return to the basement cabinet again and again to confront the Rothschild and my craving. The cabinet, surely a forgotten thing, was a dark shape against the darker concrete wall and was evocative of the alluring treasures discovered in the attic of my childhood. Helen would be dozing. Time would hang. The cabinet, with its old-wood scent, might as well have been in my childhood attic. Who was I kidding? *I* was the thing hung in time, moving, if at all, backward.

Desperate to shake this sad dawning, I would open the cabinet door, greeting the neat rows of dusty bottles. I would run my finger over them and calculate how many I might fit in my knapsack. Intrigued by this collection, moldering, forgotten, I anticipated my delight to finally get to taste a fine, cellared Bordeaux, completely untouched by conscience. Oddly, there was no switch inside my perception, as I gazed at *my* treasure, that separated my desire from my conscience. The wine was mine, and in that visceral moment, the fact that it was Helen's and that I might take what was not given bore no relation to my craving.

Helen dozed. A weak light from the tiny, square window revealed a pile of lumber earmarked, no doubt, for some Bulgarian task; broken chairs; an ancient zinc laundry tub. Something in me remembered, and I replaced the bottles that I discovered in my hand. I remembered my intent—to gaze at aging and to bring to bear an attitude of love and generosity. But here stood opposite qualities: greed and craving. To acknowledge both would have been the important thing. It would have enabled an argument and not an indulgence. I would always harbor both. It didn't sit well at first; it put a dent in my Doing-Good-and-Living-Simply image. I would go back upstairs to Helen, and we would say an affectionate and undamaged good-bye.

FOUR

⇌

Bloody Resignation

I HAD INTENDED MY PARENTS TO ADVANCE TO THE NEXT phase of their lives without me. I'd intended the work with "my" old people to connect me to my parents' aging while I remained an antiseptic 3,200 miles away. End time with Mother, according to this plan, would be a montage composed of weekly phone chats in which good memories would replace unpleasant truth, and bad memories would neutralize with distance, and peace would be made with our limitations, as I imposed images of "my" old people over Mother's narcissistic raving to thus add charm. But with every "sweetie, sweetie" imprecation, Mother turned the screw, asking, "When are you coming *home?*"

I hemmed and hawed and made excuses. I pretended I had suddenly found a "real job." I produced contingencies—a tenants' meeting coming up (that would be having a beer with Doug, my neighbor); a volunteer orientation (contingent, in turn, on finally showing up at an organization I'd intended to align with for years); recovering from a sudden bout of athlete's foot (actually, my bunion).

I knew that if I could hold my breath and let the pause that followed her plea lengthen, her panic and need would ebb and, with the Father's intervention, we'd arrive at that place in our conversation where common sense prevailed. And what made mine a tentative rejection, with flabby moral spine, was, I *could* do this. I could drop my life and go "home." I did not have the contingencies typical of a middle-aged career and family woman. I had no children, no "real job," no outstanding obligations commanding my attention. I did not even own a pet. I was free. Thus, it followed, I was free to *serve*.

After these calls, I'd hang up flooded and weak with resentment.

And then one day the Father called and said, "Your mother is in the hospital. She woke up this morning coughing blood."

That got my attention. Mimi in *La Bohème* coughed blood. Also Violetta in *La Traviata*. Chopin coughed blood. Though I had not read *The Magic Mountain*, people in that novel were said to do it, too. Okay, okay. True, *blood* made it impossible merely to enjoy Mother's hypochondria as a performance piece, say. This news unleashed many feelings, none of which were neat or tidy. They careened from horror and resentment into self-pity's wall. They chugged up the hill of regret and sorrow. They crashed again headlong into the rock face of, *Hell, no!*

Now, because I have confessed that no adult obligations stood in the way of my coming to Mother's aid, you may think that I had nothing to keep me anchored to my life. That I sat around in my little Belltown apartment, huddled on the couch, hugging my knees, in lifetime recovery from adoption and Christian Science—in short, as narcissistic and fragile as Mother. You may think I was, after all, following her career path, and couldn't I go back to Bethlehem, PA, and do that work there, as well as here?

And you may be wondering about what I actually did to support myself in this bright and blistering world. Well, I did have a life; in fact, I loved the life that I had created. How could I leave? There was just too much to do. How could I leave my turning-fifty project, the cartography of aging? How could I leave the work with "my" old people, and Harriet's kind efforts at finding me good subjects? How could I leave the challenges of menopause?

Come to think of it, I would have been thrilled to leave those hormonal hurdles.

But how could I leave Belltown? Someone had to stand by and witness as old was sacrificed to new. Someone had to honor the memory of the buildings that gave their lives to the incursion of luxury high-rise condos. Did not collective amnesia, the more typical response to this, signal the greater demise of an already history-indifferent people? How could I leave my virtuous activities—for example, the daily bike ride?

Needless to say, it would have been sticky trying to explain, in light of Mother's illness, that I couldn't betray my exercise routine. You ask, would there exist no options for exercise back there? Well, frankly, no—except for the long, tedious walk around the defunct and rotting Bethlehem Steel plant. I just knew I'd gain tremendous amounts of weight back there, and grow flabby, and start taking shallow little breaths in my parents' deathly house, and not enough oxygen would make it to my brain, and thus I would become dim-witted and totally regressed and I would be stuck in Bethlehem, PA, forever.

And then there was trapeze. I'd been waiting for an important phone call regarding this, my latest passion, for weeks. Never one to resist embracing the grandiose expression, I thought trapeze would be my last, grand turning-fifty gesture. It would also serve as a last-ditch attempt to attain grace. Even before my fifties, I was a klutz. I am the sort of person, as Mother always told me, who thinks too much, and, except when I ride my bike, I go at life from the neck up. When I was younger, I had absolutely no relationship to speak of with my feet. They were so far away they might as well have been Europe. They were little spatulas that kept me from falling fore or aft. I never even touched them. And never mind private parts. I mean, they were even farther away from me than my feet, geographically impossible though that might be.

Even though I'm older now, my brain remembers all that as my functioning reality. Yes, I have made progress. I now receive the messages both from private parts and from feet. Still, every day my brain has to go through its affirmations. *You can do this*, it says to my body, channeling my inner kinder-garten teacher. *You can do this*, it says as I stand over my sink with tucked-in tummy and deliberately relaxed knees, shoulders back, breathing deeply while I oh-so-mindfully and gracefully wash the breakfast dishes.

It was in pursuit of grace and grandiosity that I explored my learning options for trapeze. After much fishing in local university theater departments and through the Yellow Pages, I discovered a youth circus in Issaquah, some miles away, that taught classes in low-flying and static trapeze. This sounded like a safe place to start. I talked to a young youth circus graduate who was so enthusiastic about her own training that she had gone on to circus school in Florida. I asked her how it was. She responded in mixed tones of rue and excitement that did not seem connected to what she was, in the moment, doing, which was being a receptionist for the youth circus back in Issaquah.

"What are you doing back?" I asked.

"Trying to make enough money to cover all my medical bills," she answered.

This gave me pause. "I bet the training was incredibly rigorous," I said.

"I broke my ankle twice," she said, as if in alignment with my speculation that the training must have required, at the very least, Herculean effort.

"How?" I asked, imagining dizzying whirls through space and miscalculated catches.

"Walking across the parking lot," she said. "It was a really bad break."

Undeterred, I had asked the proprietor of the youth circus to kindly call me back, and that had been a week and a half earlier. As yet, she had not returned my call.

So how could I leave this imminent adventure and all my sweet routines? I could not leave my prayer. I actually said one every morning. I put in a good half hour of meditation and followed it with the Francis prayer, the one that begins, "Lord, make me an instrument of your peace. Where there is hatred, let me sow love. Where there is injury, pardon." And so forth.

I first heard this prayer on the peace walk I took with half a dozen other women. We were staying at a Trappist monastery in Nebraska, and every morning after rising, the monks and the walkers made a circle in a piney grove, held hands, and recited The Prayer of St. Francis. I loved this prayer, a prayer that made sense, because if you meant the words as you said them, it would change your life. That's what you were asking for, a spiritual adjustment, an alignment of intention with action. The prayer suggested that the heart could school the mind.

I had been saying this prayer every day for sixteen years.

And now I hear you asking, "So, *has* it changed your life?"

But don't you see? I was just too busy in my worried Belltown Buddhist writer's life to go help Mother die.

BEFORE I LEFT, I NEEDED TO TAKE A WALK. SOLID REALITY could not, in Belltown, be counted on to hold steady even in the next hour. Just a walk around the block revealed condos in progress, with names like the Concord, the Ellington, and Avalon, all springing up as fast as mushroom rings. Even before the yellow Tyvek wrapped the ascendant frames, signs declared 80 PERCENT OCCUPANCY RATE. HURRY! FEW VIEW CONDOS LEFT.

Down my street, toward Seattle Center, Italy and the myths of druidic England had seized the developers' imaginations to create a cacophony in names of epochs and fairy tales. Why such an indigestible mix? You'd think planning *might* have been afoot, for the sake of unifying the neighborhood. But no. Arthurian evocations occupied the same spatial reality and time zone of Duke Ellington, in turn a jog up the street from Alexandria, our little taste of Egypt from 332 BC. Whoever got there first seemed the organizing principle. Italy, to date, staked the lion's share of claims. In fact, for some strange reason, the Italian motif—in the realm of naming, anyway—had captured the fancy of developers for the last decade. Mind you, there is nothing reminiscent of actual Italian architecture in the design of these new buildings.

In 1996, when I moved to Belltown, it was not yet *the* place to be. Somewhat fashionable but not so relentlessly *in*, it was composed of artists' lofts, the occasional new restaurant boasting some curious blend of cuisines, the Pike Place Market, and the best hamburger joint in town. Before my little gray apartment building was made habitable, the structure, barely standing, was the home of an old drunk. The organization of architects that created a substantial number of low-income apartment buildings throughout the city bought him out and razed the decrepit house, and—presto!—put up my apartment building, to be named in honor of the old man, John Carney. It was an offense and an embarrassment to my well-shod neighbors in the Concord, the Ellington, the Avalon. Once, I overheard a real estate agent describe us, the residents of my apartment building, as "drug addicts, loonies, and artists." I was happy at last to have found my group.

Amid the condo contagion, gone was the fennel-sweetened air. Gone the glorious expanse of space as the hill fell away to the water. It had been a wonderful part of town. Gone the free play of wind and sea and weather, setting off the boutiques and the artists' lofts and the wedding-ring store and the dark and perilous corner convenience stores and the Laundromat called Sit and Spin. Gone would be the old, shanty-derivative Ivar's that stood guard at the terrifying intersection where five streets met like scattered pickup sticks. Gone the gray, multipurpose buildings whose purposes had remained obscure. Blank stares beheld the gaping holes as, blushing, we asked, "Now, what was there before?"

Some things, I knew, would never change—the terrible Tex-Mex dive called Two Dagos, where, if you dared go in, your life would be altered irretrievably and you'd find yourself walking around in Western wear, steadily increasing the circumferences of your buttocks. There would always be the missions run by Christian zealots, where the oldest, rattiest men in the world between the ages of twenty-six and sixty would line up for soup and beds. There were the artifacts of seamen culture and, on the corner across from me, the Labor Temple, as oxymoronic a name as I have ever known.

I walked by the pea patch on a lot by Elliott and Bell and marveled at the vegetable and flowerbeds flourishing between busy city streets. I climbed back up to First Avenue, past prestigious Patagonia, and marveled that just two blocks away endured the old Army Navy store, where you could still buy khaki-colored undershirts for $1. I headed toward the Pike Place Market, secure in my belief that it would be there when I returned.

Once, you could count on life in Belltown being spontaneous and unrefined. Not that I am advocating for the return of the drunken sailors and the pee-stained, matted-haired, old-young men; the unpleasant "hello, vomit" moments; or the nasty surprise of walking out to your car to find the windshield shattered. No, I do not miss those days. What I miss after a little trip away, say, is returning happily to *my* street and *my* building, to find that all of a sudden I am up on top of Queen Anne hill, wondering how the hell I got there, because all the landmarks that made my block and my building identifiable have vanished.

But what can we control, really? The more I practiced meditation, the more I realized that what I could control was my reaction to that over which I had no control. Anything else was futile, like trying to control a hot flash or, for that matter, the tone and the timing of Mother's death. Might I try to bear in mind these two phenomena in the context of surrender? Might this new way of experiencing these miseries soften my resistance and make me more generous toward myself, my menopause, and my mother?

Some women describe their hot flashes as a power surge. I experience a molten wave from my deepest core, radiating and heavy. Every pore releases this heat like a steam vent. Every half hour, my skin reenacts the formation of the Hawaiian Islands. I experience the frantic need to press myself against a cold surface, a window, chilled by the wintry night air. Even parts of me I never knew registered temperature—fingernails and foot bottoms—seek relief. Hot flashes are not my friends, leading me to inner wisdom, nor power surges, nor harbingers of my future, wise-old-woman self.

I can remember neither Mother nor Mary Baker Eddy offering guidance on such carnal female rites of passage as menstruation or menopause. Perhaps both managed to put these lifetime companions simply out of mind, reciting for example—at *that* time of month—the Scientific Statement of Being, which is as follows:

> There is no life, truth, intelligence, nor substance in matter. All is infinite Mind and its infinite manifestation, for God is All in all. Spirit is immortal Truth; matter is mortal error. Spirit is the real and eternal; matter is the unreal and temporal. Spirit is God, and man is His image and likeness. Therefore man is not material; he is spiritual.

It makes me wonder if Mary Baker Eddy menstruated, or how she framed the experience, whether she did or not. Where did she dispose of her dirty sanitary napkins, *unreal*, albeit dripping with mortal error?

I've heard women say the most audacious things: "I can't wait for menopause. I'm always cold, and hot flashes are going to make me toasty." They think menopause a celebration of lowered heating bills, or a holiday from buying expensive sweaters, or an excuse to finally parade naked around the house.

Menopause also broke my sleep. I used to love to sleep, approaching it as if it were a cavernous room in a museum, hung with paintings of John Singer Sargent or Thomas Moran —monumental, theatrical, set off in fat gold frames. Sleep used to be like that—every night promised a journey, outcome and destination unknown, through ornate golden frames. I rarely sink so deeply anymore, and if I journey, it's no farther than the bathroom, for that, too, is part of the menopause packet—the need to pee a dozen times a night.

Again, I tried to bring some Buddhist principles to these chagrins and remind myself that menopause won't last forever. Impermanence rules. Therefore, in the larger scheme of things, I might regard these years as precious. As, perhaps, I might regard Mother in her final year.

⇌

Commentary:

THE HISTORY OF MY WORK

AMONG THE MORE BECKETTIAN OF MY EMPLOYMENT opportunities, with my extensive training in Absurdism and ennui, one in particular stands out. It was to vacuum an enormous room, a cavern reserved for events—banquets and the like. The rug was vast, as fit the room, and maroon. Metal chairs, like large mammals in a diorama, lined the periphery. It was there I learned the miseries of work—specifically, miseries of the body, as if objects intended that backs be "thrown out," wrists snap, and arms ache. I was charged to vacuum the maroon rug, but no one told me how. Perhaps it should have seemed obvious, but, when facing an acreage of dark, nasty carpet, an unwieldy machine, and assaultive chairs, well, for example, how do you divide up the space so that the job makes sense?

I decided to begin at the outside wall, stumbling over the chairs, working in toward the center, and this seemed to take hours, and in that empty time, thoughts of nothingness and existential matters arose. Inside, on these late afternoons, I would pine for the outdoors. The sounds of traffic and voices and laughter would magnify my solitude as I vacuumed and I vacuumed, until it was time not to.

This experience opened me to the possibility that work was, or at least could often be, meaningless and punitive. I'd recently been expelled from Wykeham Rise, a boarding school for girls in Washington, Connecticut, presided over by Father Willoughby Newton, a towering figure. The work was my penance for my expulsion, and work would come to feel, for a long time after, like punishment rendered from on high. How these conflations dog us well beyond the signature event.

I HAVE THOUGHT OF MYSELF FOR AS LONG AS I CAN remember as a financial minimalist, a mostly underearner. I have thought of myself as poor—the writer casting out for grants; the workshop participant offering her time and labor in exchange for tuition. Regarding shelter, over the years, I'd cultivated an ingenious set of survival mechanisms. I had a talent for finding inexpensive places—safe, adequate, sometimes even free. There seems, for example, to have been a whole decade of house sitting. Or I could always qualify for, if not actually arts *money*, then arts *housing*—although officially categorized as "low-income housing for recovering addicts, mental health patients, and artists." I lived, in that context, for five years in an apartment whose handicapped bathroom was as large as the apartment itself, about 360 square feet total. I was happy there, as I had been in all my modest places, all my "deals." I paid $225 a month for my lunatic, addict, artist housing.

I have managed never to be homeless, although I have squatted in hovels—four years on an island in Puget Sound in a shred of un-insulated, unplumbed cabin. An outhouse; water in a jug on a make-do stand; firewood gleaned from blowdown, split, stacked, and seasoned.

⇌

"WHAT DO YOU DO?" IS A QUESTION THAT HAS ALWAYS made me cringe. There were never easy answers. I envied those for whom there were: "I am a doctor/a teacher/a landscape architect." Those answers led naturally to further questions, and further out into pastures of rolling conversation. I sweated for my answer, struggling to find a concrete correspondence in abstract qualities—humor, curiosity, imagination, pluck. On the other hand, "What have I done?" triggers far less comparison-induced anxiety, as the act of reflection tends to make substance and meaning even out of failure. Perhaps it is because I feel mine—writing—to be a useless occupation while remaining the only thing that marshals my errant thoughts and chthonic feelings and drifting bits of identity toward meaning.

"What do you do?" is typically answered not by a verb but a noun. "I am a [blank]" offers myriad opportunities for me to compare my flakiness with your solid mass. There is still no easy answer. I have a BA in fine arts and an MA in English—American romanticism, to be exact. For what have these equipped me?

It did not occur to me until I was in my fifties that making a living and making literature—poems, plays, essays, memoirs, and one or two "failed" novels—were separate endeavors. They might relate, but rarely, and for those for whom they did, genius, stamina, luck, and some kind of supportive community were requisite. That it did not occur to me to give up this hope, this dream, until middle age was upon me is noteworthy. How could I not have grasped this sooner?

THERE IS THE SPIRITUAL COMPONENT TO WORK, SET FORTH in the Buddhist Noble Eightfold Path—Right Livelihood:

may one's work harm no one and nothing, and contribute to the well-being of others, even if those others reside in the realm of carrots and lettuces. There is the Freudian component —work as an apex of the realized self, and the cultivation of qualities such as grace and brace in the trenches of competition; collaborative bonhomie; intellectual engagement that lifts one beyond the pulls of leisure and rest; even toward food and water.

Mine, though, has stayed at a kind of sixth-grade level of achievement. You work very hard at a modest job—bagging groceries, carrying the mail—and create its meaning on the side. Meaning and work and money, in this scheme, are not equal partners, although in my father's case, they were. I learned new details that accrued to his character in the memorial services after his death. His graduate students, now old men themselves, attested to my father's love of his work and his encouragement of their endeavors: "It's not enough to love what you do. There's no reason why your work shouldn't make you a lot of money."

This was a shocker. My frugal dad, the courtly, quiet engineer: "Make money, boys!" Why did it not occur to him to sit me down kindly, as he did with my algebra phobia, and help me understand the connection between my getting a paper route, say, and acquiring my very own comic-book collection?

WORK IS HARD TO DEFINE SUCCINCTLY, LIKE A HIKE UP from a lush mountain valley to above the tree line. Does one focus on the dank underbrush and the challenge of solid footing; the brief glimpses of blue sky between the one-thousand-year-old hemlocks, firs, and cedars teasingly seen;

the piney, mineral-laced air; or on the fact that one is panting and the incline is not *that* steep, so when did *that* happen? My feelings and thoughts about work are many and varied.

My work has been revealed through projects having nothing to do with income and rarely with employment. Like the zoo. Like walking.

MY FAVORITE JOB IN LIFE WAS WORKING AT THE Franklin Park Children's Zoo in Boston. I moved there after college with my friend and love, Nancy B. Shortly after we set up our apartment on Massachusetts Avenue, we began to pore over the classifieds every morning, in search of jobs. As we sat on the bare wooden floor of our apartment, a thin, frayed American flag hanging in the tall, single-paned window that rattled in the bracing wind, I fantasized about working at the circus. Was there one? After all, I knew two girlhood friends who had "run off and joined the circus"—one a clown, the other a feathered, dangling girl. Then, as ever, I was drawn more toward the exotic than to solid, practical *career-path* kinds of work. No, here in Boston, there was no circus. But there was the zoo. On a whim, I called. "Yes," I was told, "there is seasonal work. We're hiring."

I was hired as the dietician, Nancy B. as the elephant mother. Even though our jobs could not have paid more than minimum wage and our employment would end only four months later, in October, these disadvantages did not deter.

What would a fine arts major bring to an occupation at the zoo? What would one bring of Rembrandt or Beethoven, Jane Austen, Samuel Beckett, Gertrude Stein? The delight in observation, I suppose.

The children's zoo exhibited *baby* animals: the *baby* Bengal tigers, Roger and Elizabeth; Nancy B.'s ward, Little Ton; the pumas; the *baby* woolly monkeys, Rufus and Debbie; the tiny spider monkey, Kim. There was a central rotunda with glass-fronted cages containing a baby llama and, across the way, a not-very-baby-at-all boa constrictor, fed live chicks every few days. We would gather, horrified and giddy, to watch the graceful dance of boa and prey—the snake rising slowly from its fat coil, regarding the chick with icy eye; the slow dawning of the chick, frozen there, to its fate; its awful last moments of chick life; and then a pair of feet dangling from the snake's jaw, the chick lump worked through the snaky tunnel. Oh, the arresting, lively drama.

The mornings, even in the terrible slum of Dorchester, the zoo's neighborhood, dawned rosy and clear—too early for despair, too early for oppressive weather. The magic of that small park commenced well before the gates were open to the public. The animals would have been up and stirring since dawn. From the vaulted, outdoor aviary came screeches and caws, coos and warbles. The gibbons howled eerily as they flung themselves through the air from the intricate bars of the jungle gym on their concrete island. The atmosphere thrummed with roars and snufflings and simian giggles, the stomping of the emus at their dance, like Toulouse-Lautrec chorus girls, all dust and tulle. What public would ever get to see Cassie, a lithe, long-haired college girl walking "her" Bengal tigers, Roger and Elizabeth, on the grounds of the waking zoo? Looking back, I wonder how it was even possible that this happened—a beautiful young woman walking "her" tigers in this somewhat paradise, protected from the Boston slum. How was it no one was mauled or eaten? One might as well have stumbled on a unicorn reclining on the lap of a virgin.

First to arrive at the front gates were the mounds and piles of various feeds and foods that we loaded onto hand trucks and wheelbarrows. There were the heavy, reinforced cartons of "feline diet," long tubes of leaking, bloody mash. There were the tubs of smelt and herring for the otters; crates of fruit—overripe citrus, rotting bananas, kiwis, and grapes—for the feces-smearing chimpanzees; giant plastic packages of baby-elephant formula.

There were certainly irritants (the crowds), protocol, rules and rivalries, and schedules, routine visits from the vet for routine upsets, but in and around the administrative tasks, eccentricities abounded: blonde Connie, the other dietician, who loved to French-kiss Rufus the woolly monkey, his tongue muscular and black; my new friend Phoebe, pale and naive and teasable, who, when Boston nightlife was discussed, believed that to be a magazine; Nancy B., fiercely protective of her elephant ward, whom she bathed with a long, stiff-bristle broom, fed from a five-gallon jug, and marched around the zoo *after* Roger and Elizabeth had completed their perambulation.

We were bathed in the endless possibilities suggested by these mornings in the first few months of graduation from our tiny Midwestern women's college, and buoyed before the realization hit, and bludgeoned: *All I have studied has no practical application here, in Boston, Massachusetts; hence, in the real world. I have cultivated a mind but not an occupation. I cannot even type.*

Nevertheless, exposure to the wildness, the hopeful morning air, the animals rustling on their straw in their cleaned cages, the odor of feed and excrement, the sounds of breathing, a whiff of sweat on the haunch of a ruminant. . . .

What a privilege to have worked at the zoo. I would forever remain a minion to these sensory delights.

Monastery

WORK CAN RELATE TO SPIRITUAL CALLING. ONE EXEMplifying experience sticks in mind: a peace walk called On the Line. We were seven women. It was the spring of 1984. Our work was walking from the Bremerton Submarine Base in Washington state to the Pantex plant in Amarillo, Texas, twenty miles a day, in order to "out" the white train that carried the warheads that armed Trident nuclear submarines. The train had been crisscrossing the country from Amarillo, west to Bremerton, and east to Charleston, South Carolina, in strict secrecy to weapons storage areas (WSAs) around the nation for thirty-six years. It traveled at night through rural communities at perilously high speeds. Our walk intended to link the communities along the tracks through programs and potlucks and media coverage and, when our paths crossed that of the white train, to hold silent vigils.

The train was watched very carefully by a knot of activists outside the plant in Amarillo, and when it was ready to leave, a cross-country vigil would be set in motion with a phone call from the vigilers. Many in "our" towns, which were roughly twenty miles apart, would pour out. They would walk in silence to the tracks, carrying candles, placards and signs, pets and babies. Our work was to encourage a citizenry to gather in loving observance.

How did we get by? I remember small pouches of cash— lunch money, donations from the road, and those sent from our Seattle coordinators. I remember my lover's credit card cut

up in a small Midwestern bank before her astonished eyes—
her lifeline snapped. I remember gifts of shoes and chocolate,
an arrangement for a weeklong retreat in an old Boy Scout
camp in the Laramie Mountains of Wyoming.

Our work—proselytizing, being open to the elements—
depended on the kindness of others. We were greeted as
heroes or shrill Cassandras, seven women walking "alone" for
peace. Many perceived us thus, the "alone" referring to the fact
that we had no men with us, overlooking the obvious, which
was that we had each other. Our twenty miles a day covered
Washington, Oregon, Idaho, Wyoming, Nebraska, Kansas,
Oklahoma, and Texas. The walk was defined by structure—up
at dawn, pack the carts, eat breakfast, set out along the tracks
to the next town—and each day defined by footsteps and miles
and the vast, often exquisite country and the strange evolution
of our animosities and allegiances, which surged and hardened
into an unfortunate dynamic. This was our work.

I would write a book, and so I'd say, for many years, that
the peace walk was my work, from the early planning phases—
as our group haggled and perspired around a pinewood table—
through the book's completion, which culminated in a PEN/
Jerard Fund award in 1992. Maybe eight years total. This was
my work. What did I do for money? The two—my work and
my money—simply didn't relate.

When it ended—and the day would come, although I
would quit the walk several times, always to return—when it
actually ended, I was told by Rhea, she who was the source of
all things holy, about a Benedictine monastery in Abiquiu,
New Mexico—Christ in the Desert—where, years ago, she had
retreated. I determined to go there. I thumbed rides. A strange
refrain came to mind: "walk until there is no fear." I didn't

know what had to be worked out of my system. Was it walking away from the collective, from the group, from the clang and chatter, its animosities and throb? It was October, beginning to get cold. I'd scraped together a pile of inadequate provisions. I don't remember the rides, only that I got them, and the refrain, which might have portended my murder. After all, "walk until there is no fear" points in two directions: either death, and that will be that, or a walk in faith, to take what comes as a blessing.

And suddenly we were driving through Abique and there were mesas and a Georgia O'Keeffe landscape all around. The driver stopped at a slight rise and the soil was red clay, and there had been gumbo, because of the autumn rains. There was a red path through the red rise pitching downward, toward a canyon, and there was a river, and he said, "Keep the river on your left; the monastery is thirteen miles in."

It was evening. It had taken a day to get here. I had a bit of water. I remember my thin cotton pants and my provisions, lashed together as if I were a mendicant from an earlier time. I clutched a plastic bag containing what may have been Chinese takeout, my sleeping bag and pad strapped to my shoulders. Night would fall soon, and darkness, although there was a moon. I walked, keeping the river, the Chama, on my left. It was a slow, narrow river there, and when I'd gone far enough into the canyon and come to an incline with a bit of flat ground, I stopped and made camp. No fire. It was high desert and getting colder.

I passed an endless night, rich in the variety of discomforts—pebbled, sandy ground and divots; the cold; the moon, too bright to sleep; the certainty that resident fauna would eat me.

I awoke the next morning, or at least stiffly uncurled from

my frozen shape, scraped together my provisions, resumed walking, thirteen miles. *Keep the river on your left.* A car appeared. I felt it. Good morning, we said. His name was Tom; he retreated here every year, he said. "I will tell them you are coming." I had rejected his offer of a ride. "They always save a room for walk-ins."

I was a walk-in. There was a name for who and what I was. He said, "There is a fork in the road. Take the right one. I will draw you an arrow."

And it was here that all of the days of my walking struck me in the heart as kindness. Above Abique, it struck me in that way. Everything that happened—broken shoes and friendships; vigils with strangers and the camaraderie risen from a single political focus; chocolate and its lack; illness— over all the vagaries spread kindness, which had brought me here, to my place that was waiting with the monks. You are not paid for this, but sometimes they will save you a place.

I walked. Early morning warmed to ten o'clock. I thought I smelled fresh bread baking. The river on my left remained chattery and shallow. The mesas loomed ahead to the right, as if I were walking downhill into a pink and chalk-white vale. Tom's arrow, big as a Cadillac, signaled straight ahead, and there, in the near distance, I saw a cluster of low adobe build-ings, maroon-ish against the sandy earth; the bell tower of the chapel; the shop where the Benedictines sold their crafts and texts.

I walked through the gate toward the building adjacent to the chapel, following the smell of baking bread. I climbed some stairs and found myself talking to an aproned monk with flour on his nose, who answered, "Oh, yes, we were expecting you."

I was shown my cell. I had all that was needed: a narrow shelf with a narrow pad and blanket for my bed; a desk with solid, fragrant wood; a lantern; a stove with piñon kindling and logs; a window. It was one of a dozen cells clustered and scattered along the river. Did I pray? I believe so. And to whom? There was a niche in the chapel for Mary; the brothers seemed to privilege Mary in their thanks.

When all of it was over—the walk, the monastery, the long trek home—my work was to make a transition from fervid collectivity to solitude, from extraordinary pilgrimage to the quotidian, from activist to earner, and this was hard, possibly harder than the walk itself. Being in one's life, in the groove of it, requires feeling secure—security, safety, attachment. In Mary's softened corner, amid the play of candlelight on the dark maroon of the adobe walls, these feelings hovered, coming to rest my anxious heart. But I had left my safe corner and the vivid life of the walk, returning to the ordinary world. And in that world, security is predicated on having money.

It is not as if the brothers turned their backs on the monetary and the material. They were Benedictines. They produced their crafts and sold them in the gift shop. The garden fed their community. They were immersed in the surrounding earth; their chapel looked raked into form from the rough tumble of the mesas. It was not as if the earth did not inform the worship. The earth nourished it. Their worship was rooted in place—river, cottonwoods, tamarisks, melons and squash in the garden, mesas, raptors soaring overhead. Nothing abstract or disembodied about the practice of their faith. But in the monastery the question of one's worth with regard to money was suspended in favor of one's occupation, prayer, and contemplation. Each brother had his work. One might bake, another tend the garden. Hoes and spades, rolling pins—rudimentary tools. There might not even have been a telephone.

So, for a while, my work was to wander. I thought of myself in that way. It is odd to think how religion and God and faith are, in small proportion, requisites for respectability, and yet, blow them up, live the principles, test God and faith, put yourself in the brew, literally, and respectability falls away. One becomes suspect, other.

WHILE ON A WALK AROUND ONE OF SEATTLE'S POPULAR neighborhood parks, Green Lake, I saw, among the more usual perambulating phenomena, a man sporting a crisp, chestnut-colored, long-sleeved shirt with matching baseball cap and no pants whatsoever—as in nothing, not even underwear or a thong. He dangled a large sign at hip level: FREE HUGS, KISSES—NO OBLIGATION. SELF-DETERMINATION. I couldn't read the rest. The moment passed too fast. There followed shock and absorption.

Perhaps the nearly naked man, his neat little bare buns bobbing out of view, was enacting his personal "take" on self-determination around the three-mile lake periphery. Was his intent to promulgate Hobbes? To demonstrate the right of the individual, the natural equality of all men, and a liberal interpretation of law that leaves people free to do whatever the law does not explicitly forbid? Wasn't there a law against bare, bobbing buns open to the public?

There was something touching and terrible about the nearly naked man. Was it his presumption that his kisses and hugs would be welcomed? Was it the whiff of learnedness that self-determination suggested? What did that mean, anyway, in the light of hugs and kisses? Was it his pressed sport shirt and matching cap, as if careful thought had been given to the top part and equally careful attention to the bottom, but this to disturbing effect? Was it his gait, brisk and unflinching? Who could not have seen, immediately, from fifty feet away that something was seriously not right? Who would not instantly have imagined how it must feel to take one's genitals walking, letting the breeze lift and play and tickle? And who would have accepted the offer of a nearly naked hug? Would the hug be chaste, each pelvic area observing a discreet distance? How would the inequality of the private parts be addressed?

What does this have to do with my work life?

That I have always desired my work to be received as an offering; that this was rarely so; that, thus, I would retreat, mute and naked.

F I V E

⇌

Role Reversal

I WAS MADE QUEASY BY THE PUDDLE OF THE SELF THAT
had become my mother. Perhaps my attachment to the hope of
aging well was predicated on its more typical improbability.
Perhaps this signature birthday of mine offered only the first
taste of aging's flavors as Mother continued to ripen. In any
event, I struggled to cultivate compassion in the face of her
increasing helplessness, her poor, ever-diminishing limpness,
her beseeching phone calls.

On one trip back, the Father picked me up, as usual, at the
airport. It was very late. Veils of mist clung to the thick
branches of the trees, barren of foliage. It all lay strewn and
scattered over the slick streets—heaps of yellow, orange, and
deep-red leaves, glistening and flattened. The dark, hulking
Gothic mansions that characterized this part of town took our
silent ride several notches closer to gloom. After our grave
hellos, the Father and I sat swaddled in the thick, leathery
quiet of his Cadillac. It was dark, midnight dark, and drizz-

ling, and I didn't know what to expect at the hospital. The thing about my father's method of communication was that he didn't make the connection between the contents of his head and working the material out through his mouth, so I had to ask questions continuously—how bad really was it, and what about the blood, and had the test results come back? Finally I gave up trying to talk and settled for trying to read his mind.

The hospital floor had a sleepy, tucked in-feel. I followed the Father down the corridor, dreading the moment of seeing the tiny Mother in her bed. I hadn't seen her for two years. Then, even extending an arm or holding up a book had been the equivalent of two sets of fifteen reps with twenty-pound weights. She had wobbled with fatigue, and her face had loomed over her eighty-pound frame like a moon-shaped mask. Even back then she'd become an old woman, grown impossibly older.

I peeked through the curtain that closed off her private room. She lay on her bed, palms up, in a demeanor of sweet waiting, and her eyes lit up when she saw me. A clear green oxygen tube bisected her face. My mother's physicality had all but burned away. What was left flickered, a votive's tiny flame.

She wore a green velvet bathrobe with gold trim. It was oddly festive, as if she had gift-wrapped herself for the hospital stay. Her pale skin covered the planes and juttings of her face lightly, like a sheet. Each breath rasped, as if breathing dried her out. Her mouth gaped open. The jaw had lost its hinges. Her breathing sounded like she'd blown out her air sacs. When she inflated her poor lungs, the air leaked out of them. I put down my suitcase. I did not want to be bigger and stronger and more able than this reduction of Mother to an essence of skin and breath and bone. I did not want to be a mother to my mother. This was not my job.

"How are you, Mum?" I asked into her lit-up smile, and let myself feel glad to see her. Her fragility was making it hard to cling to pouting as my major attitude.

She concentrated on trying to answer my question as if she were a little girl asked what state, alphabetically, follows Delaware.

"Robert," she said, searching for him through my body, "tell her how I am." Her face suddenly cracked open. She started coughing and gestured frantically toward one of a dozen boxes of tissues. After several racking efforts, she spat into a pink tissue. She held it out like an offering. Her eyes filled with wonder. Having expelled a plop of blood the size of a silver dollar, she fell back into the waiting cushions of her bed. I felt its squishy warmth through the thin tissue. I peeked. The blood wasn't bloody colored but rather maroon. Viscous, it had retained its silver-dollar shape. I looked at Mother and the Father solemnly, as—worried—they looked back at me.

I offered to stay the night, thinking to be of use while at the same time terrified I'd catch what Mother had—this chronic pulmonary disease related to tuberculosis. Wasn't a mere cough enough to annihilate whole colonies of people?

The Father left after making sure that the nurse would find me a cot, but the hospital, despite all of its sophisticated machinery, comforting beeps, and pleasant staff, was allotted one cot for every floor, and someone else's emergency was in it. I was offered the reclining chair. It had an ailing mechanism, which pitched me forward with every subtle shift of my position. The nurse warned me not to let my head touch the headrest, "Because," she said, "one never knows." But after the long flight, the hospital felt merely an extension of the airplane. There was the same mechanically generated air, the dizzying lack of options for recreation or release, the hushed atmosphere of a sealed capsule transporting bodies through space and time.

The next morning Mother was given a drug to drain her lungs, warned that a regrettable side effect throughout the day would be long, voluminous pees. The physiological connection between draining her lungs and filling her bladder would remain a conundrum. The Father was working his crossword puzzle, taking his turn in the nasty chair. Now, just because we didn't trust each other, and just because we weren't healthfully attached, didn't mean I wasn't hungry for her love, and so I took the opportunities my mother's decrepitude created to touch her, now waving furiously, the need to pee upon her.

Heeding her urgent cries, I leveraged her out of bed, as the oxygen tubing, malignant and vile as the reclining chair, hissed, snaking, underneath our feet. Holding both her hands, I backed up, as if leading her into my embrace. We shuffled and hobbled and achieved the bathroom. Step by tiny step, I pivoted her bottom toward the toilet and aimed. I pulled her robe up, pulled her panties down, and lowered her sad, hanging buttocks onto the special insert designed to collect this special pee from her draining lungs.

I was having an intimate moment with Mother's bottom. Not that Mother's bottom could honestly be called a proper *bottom*. There was her sacrum, a cuttlebone-shaped mound over which was draped some flesh. There were the soft draperies of her buttocks, baby soft, smelling sweet, like powder. I smiled, remembering Mother's odd pronunciation for body-part words. She had always called this bottom properly by its "buttocks" term, pronouncing the two syllables roundly and distinctly. "Butt-tox," she'd sing out.

I lowered my mother and her butt-tox onto the toilet seat. I squatted beside her and stroked her hand. She let her head fall upon her palms, leaning into her exhaustion. Her hair, thin and washed with a shampoo powder, rose and fell away with my breath. The bones of her shoulders stuck up through her happy robe.

Collapsed in this position. I couldn't interpret the little "ohs" that escaped with each exhale. I did not know, because this was my first time to be the mother of my mother, and because a greater fondness for denial compromised her capacity for truth. I reached over her narrow lap to grab some toilet paper for my weepy eyes. "I have to blow my nose," I said to the flat back of her head, bowed over her lap, as if in prayer. I was on my knees beside her, in the perfect posture for saying the Francis prayer. The wheel of life had made a quarter turn. I was tending Mother's bottom as, fifty-some years ago, she had tended mine.

We completed the ordeal and shuffled back to bed, and there was the doctor. He sat cross-legged on the wastebasket, a foot dangling loosely off one knee. He asked about Mother's coughing: Had there been less blood? I told him she'd been coughing, had produced half a dozen globs. His expression turned grave. The Father was not there.

"It's not working," he said, betraying alarm. Mother slumped in her recliner and couldn't hear a thing. "What do you think we should do?" he asked me, and took my hand. Now, *that* was discouraging.

"My father needs to know that it's not working," I said, not understanding what should be working but wasn't. "They have to decide together what to do." This was what I understood: her disease, chronic, had been treated with a powerful cocktail of four antibiotics. These made her dreadfully sick. The choice not to take her medicine was the lesser of two evils. Taking it meant constant nausea and not eating, when she was already skin and bone. Not taking it meant that the disease would progress more quickly.

Now, understand, Mother lived to eat. Her aptitude for food exceeded the satisfaction of simple need in ways that produced a wily antidote to all that physical denial that Christian Science enhanced. So, even though she looked as fragile as a baby bird, and even though eating itself often required more stamina than she could muster, to have food withdrawn as *the* organizing principle in her life would have killed her more quickly than her actual disease.

By the time the Father returned from his walk, a nurse was helping Mother have her fifth Olympic pee. I told him about my conversation with the doctor—that she would decline irreversibly were she not to take the antibiotics. He listened gravely, open in the moment to any possibility that would seem to make her better, while struggling against the realization that she *wouldn't* get better, and he suffered a brief facial spasm and then turned red.

"Will you write your mother's obituary?" he asked, his little-boy eyes lost and brimming. You might think that for me, the writer and the daughter (both states observed so meagerly in the Father's value system), this was something to make both feel honored, and that in his world, it would be regarded as a simple thing—you grab a little anecdote to illustrate both views and values of the dearly departed and sprinkle in the usual "who-how-whens." On the contrary, such a request was huge. These were the reasons:

a) I did not know my mother, or at least know enough complimentary things to say about her.

b) I couldn't think of anything complimentary to say.

c) The "truth" about my mother, as I perceived it, and the Father's adoration of his wife presented a discrepancy the walls of which were so tall, you'd need Superman and Supergirl to scale it.

On the other hand, here he sat in the wretched chair, crying. I had never seen the Father cry. Such wrenching moments make one agree to incongruous things.

All of these new experiences were making me very tired. I could barely hold myself up. First Mother's bottom, now her obituary. Added to which, her passivity cast a spell on me. Now, any feminist worth her salt loathes passivity, and so I am ashamed to admit that every time Mother was patted and pet, fed and falsely reassured, rubbed, combed, and oiled, my contempt tipped its hat to envy. When we lifted her for a wash or a feed, she fell into a pose of ecstatic martyrdom. Her bony chest was bared; her head lolled back from her shoulders, as if she'd been lifted off the cross. Plus, she almost always slept. Where did she go in sleep? I wondered could I follow? Her sleep called out to me. *Meet me here*, it said, *in darkness, in drifting*. Perhaps our sleep would ferry us to such alluring places where we'd say things that we could never say before.

As if reading my mind, Mother opened her eyes and looked at me. "It isn't as easy to love as you think it's going to be," she said. I looked at her, not understanding. What was she saying? Admittedly, I kept slipping between a kind of hyper-alert, über-functioning and a trance-like state, so I well might have hallucinated this strange disclosure. Was this an end-time gem? I held my breath, wanting more, wanting details to pin onto her experience. Was it a reference to the adoption, to how difficult it was for her, initially, to love *me*? I leaned forward, struggling to engage her eyes, but whatever shades and shadows had prompted the disclosure had turned another corner in her mind, and her eyes rolled back, closing.

How, like Mother, I was craving sleep. Like Mother, I wanted just to lie, sunk underneath my covers—a lump of passive receipt, *being* patted, *being* stroked and fed and tended. She'd found a way to let go of striving. Here was Ophelia, the senior version.

Here was *vocation*. Here was raison d'être. She suffered no shame in this. Quite the opposite, decline inspired a whole new set of coping skills. Her favorite subjects remained her health and what she'd had for lunch. Over the past dozen years, my assignment had been to soothe and to encourage, and initially I had been flattered that she shared her fears with me. But fear as a refrain left too long unattended is suspect in the end. What were her fears serving? Mother's lack of interest in her psychological relationship to her ailments made me reach, many a time, for a glass of bracing chardonnay.

As you may have ascertained, I had trouble accepting Mother's illness as, well, *real* somehow. For decades, if not longer, before achieving her diagnosis, she paddled among a variety of lesser ailments. For a while, it was insidious "phlegm" that plagued her, enhanced by lactose intolerance, osteoporosis, and the unassuagable cough. Her pursuit of physicians, experts, and caregivers occupied much time. I couldn't help but think that Mother had entered the Realm of Illness sumptuously, fully devoting herself to the consumption of care.

This flew in the face of my belief that everyone's suffering, however it looks on the outside, is real to the one inside it. But illness seemed her currency, her method for extracting love.

HOW FINE, IN THESE SITUATIONS, TO HAVE RELIGION. Although Mother remained an avid devotee of Christian Science, leavening its dense obscurity with Fundamentalist Christian claptrap, she had consented to join the Father's Congregationalist church, a less byzantine Christian sect. Regarding the protocol of death, my parents needed help with the how-to's and so sought a church's counsel.

The minister of the Father's church was named, with Dickensian adroitness, Reverend Quail, and he had come to visit. I shook his offered hand, warm and reassuringly plump, but I pressed my lips together, wanting it understood that I would buy no Christian pap. His small feet ended in soft Italian pumps. Mother and the Reverend chatted in the way that the sick and the officious do, and then she got it in her head to pray.

She called us to her from the menacing recliner—the Father, the minister, and me. With fluttering hands, she indicated that we must make a circle, and so, gathering, we joined hands. Reverend Quail launched into the generic "Dear Lord, we ask that You comfort Your child, Elizabeth, in her time of need." It went on for a long time, and then Mother was inspired to make a prayer of her own, and, still holding hands, we began swaying from side to side. She told Jesus how much she loved him and asked that he let her go home, cured, and then she thanked God the Father for her many blessings. This prayer exceeded Reverend Quail's in length. Her requests grew specific—rest and a reliable cleaning woman for Robert; a haircut and a winter coat for me. Then she said how grateful she was to be surrounded by her loving family, even though the two people in it—the Father and me—hardly made a wagon train.

When she finished her prayer, she asked for a farewell prayer from the reverend. It was clear that he'd run out of inspiration, although he still had some clichés at the ready. When he finished, Mother took his other hand and begged him, as she begged everyone, to come back and see her soon. She kept going in and out of thinking that she was hosting a party.

"How about a hug?" he asked. He bent over her like a large forest mammal, tripped, pitched toward her chair, and sent her cane clattering to the floor. Since I had begun working with the old people, I had been noticing how canes inspired odd behavior. I had got to thinking that I could write a little pamphlet on cane protocol, as I was always on the lookout for career opportunities. Quail recovered his composure, drew her toward him in his mammalian embrace, and then turned and tiptoed from the room. A look of relief passed across his face as he left us. We were alone again, Mother's Perfect Family, and she looked at the Father and me and beamed and asked, "Now, who in the world was *that*?"

After three days going on a year, my visit ended. I gazed down at Mother in her bed, about to say good-bye. I memorized the details of her fragile package—the bold topography of her bones, unencumbered by fat or muscle; the fluttering breath, like butterflies trapped inside her chest; her amazingly stiff, stand-up hair. I would not forget this body in its final year. I touched her face with a damp washcloth, pressing gently on her eyes, into the folds of her ears, and against her slack jaw. She lifted her face toward the cloth, surrendering.

I leaned over her, trying to read some clear message in her eyes. Did she know this was good-bye? There had been more good-byes than I thought possible in these three days. Each small task that I performed for her required its own farewell. I'd bathed and fed my mother, helped hoist the flesh hanging off her tired bones, settled her on the potty and wiped her bottom. I'd touched her as if I were the mother, she the babe.

I realized that until Mother died, my days and how I lived them were up for grabs. "Good-bye," I whispered. "I love you." I said good-bye to all of her retreating powers, and "I love you" slipped out, along with the astonishing and utterly unforeseen "I'll miss you."

She rallied. She roused. "When are you coming back?" she snapped, clear-eyed. Her hands strained toward mine.

SIX

⇌

Identity and Other Foolish Matters

WHEN I GOT BACK FROM BETHLEHEM, PA, THERE HAD been a celebrity sighting. I myself had yet to experience such a thing in my neighborhood. In my brief time away, the wealthy and well shod had taken up residence in the new condo building next door. There were telltale props: glossy SUVs, fashion-statement dogs, pursed "kiss me" lips on the women, the arrogance of hurry. The neighborhood had been jolted from its easy, unself-conscious day-to-day, and I felt subsequently and chafingly aware of my *un*wealthy and *un*celebrity (i.e., nonentity) status.

This mournful comeuppance was enhanced by another neighborhood phenomenon, whom I'll call Trish. The night of my return from Mother, I spotted her in Larry's, the "you can get everything your heart desires" store where I grocery-shop. She walked by the deli counter carrying several mangoes, a jug of milk, and a bag of corn chips in her arms. Common, ordinary things. I mention this because Trish did common, ordinary things in an uncommon and extraordinary manner. For example, walking. She did not just fall into a certain functional gait that carried her across a street or down a set of stairs. She scanned. Her eyes riveted on the ground a few feet ahead, as if she were looking for her mother's diamond ring that had managed to fall off her finger moments before. This point, this "perhaps" ring, drew her forward with unswerving deliberation. Her head was a bloodhound, hot on a scent trail. And all the while a cigarette was going, and she held it as if it were a device to ward off malarial mosquitoes. This little jog through Larry's suggested that she'd had some basic training in the ways of nurturance and self-care.

Trish was lean, with a thickly tangled veil of hair, its color the same color as her face—gray and brown. She was a gray-brown woman from tip to toe. When the weather turned warm, she would sit outside the coffee shop, or upstairs from Larry's at a green metal table, gesturing with her cigarette and leaning this way and that, into and away from that which she was speaking to or with. She soliloquized. I had eavesdropped on these speeches, often a mix of verbs and obscenities. One such involved testicles and someone shoving them into someone else's face, reported with a great deal of animated indignation.

I watched Trish very carefully. The week before, I had gone up to Larry's at noon, when I knew she'd be soliloquizing. There she'd sat, her spine straight as a pole from which she bent and swayed. She was gesturing in a grand fashion, using her cigarette as a kind of conductor's baton. She waved it grandly, as if making many points, each needing its particular emphasis. She was a regular performance piece, my Trish, sitting dancer-erect but with limbs sibilant and reedlike in syncopation with the gist of her rant. For rant it was, as I inched closer, catching phrases of obscenity—a free-asso-ciation riff on the theme of the *male part*—she hardly paused for breath. Her posture reminded me of a muscular little girl's —I could almost feel the two hard columns on either side of her spine. Hers was a body unpadded by the roundness life bestows on many women. As people passed, crossing her line of vision, her eyes followed them without engaging while her mouth rattled on and on. She talked, in this way, to any who crossed her line of vision, while engaging no one. She seemed quite at home in the world like this.

What for God's sake do Trish and celebrity sightings have to do with your mother? you will ask. It is the foolish matter of identity.

I HAVE ALWAYS THOUGHT MYSELF ENVIOUS OF OTHERS, desiring an idealized Self, more adorable, more solid than this self of mine. This began quite early. I remember sitting at my little maple desk in my parents' home in Bethlehem. I must have been in high school. It was the year *Hello, Dolly!* stormed Broadway, and for some reason that completely defies logic, I had fallen in love with Carol Channing. My love did not confine itself merely to the acquisition of album and poster. No, I wrote her a proposal in which I stated my desire to devote my mundane, boring little life to serving her. *Serving*, I kid you not. I was sixteen and already versed in self-attrition. I offered to be her secretary or her dresser—something that would have legitimized the love. I was casting about, even then, to be Somebody, not even *somebody else*, for that implies that you already have a somebody that you want to trade in for an *else*. I know, I know—Carol Channing does not come to mind as one of those individuals who will go down in history as terribly important, even though she is, or was, a Christian Scientist, which certainly added heft.

Carol Channing was adored for being, well, odd and eccentric, and in our sort-of family, any oddness, any cracks, in our polite, cunningly deflective, bland exteriors inspired dread and terror, and so examples of the odd and the eccentric offered me an out. Behaviors that veered away from the convention-bound Stout tried and true were called You Are Emotionally Disturbed. It was a capital-letter condition that required medication and lockup.

To my Carol Channing query letter, I received a reply. It said something like: *Miss Channing appreciates the offer, but perhaps you'd better finish growing up and then we'll see.* Gently, it suggested that certain skills might make my offer more appealing. Like typing. Experience with PR. What I didn't know was that I didn't really want to be Ms. Channing's personal secretary so much as I wanted to be Ms. Channing, she of the raspy voice and adorable eccentricity. I wanted quite simply to own a self that was adored. I looked around my world, and everybody had one, and how did a self get acquired?

When I was a playwright, with enough of a self both to start a theater in Philadelphia and to cultivate a drinking problem while living in a suburban garage, I wanted to be Virginia Woolf. This did not improve my writing. It made it pretentious and abstract, and my friends accused me of elitism. I even dressed like Woolf—in sweeping skirts and old gray cardigans with punched-out pockets. I stopped short at wearing rocks inside the pockets, though.

I don't know if I genuinely coveted the identity of our newest Belltown celebrity, but I knew absolutely, albeit sadly, that I did not want, and would never want, to be Trish. I say "sadly" because I cannot imagine anybody loving Trish for being herself. Can you? It would take Oliver Sacks to make Trish's an imaginable way of being in the world and to neutralize it with compassion.

Identity as a pursuit—what a bane; what an influenza. It is not fixed; it is shifting. It is Trish, pursuing the scent of her self while crossing the street, cigarette smoke trailing behind her. Yet how we cling. I think Mother was afflicted by identity angst, too, and in the end it made her so very tired. My mother created herself from scratch—a poor girl without a father, from Reading, Pennsylvania, earning half a business-school degree, who, over the years, because of her husband's career successes, turned herself into A Lady. Yes, Mother was A Lady, an apt choice for one who sought protection. Maybe she became exhausted by the perceived need to self-generate in every single moment—as did I. We had that in common.

⇌

Commentary:

BETHLEHEMPENNSYLVANIA

EACH TIME CONSCIENCE FORCED ME TO RETURN TO Bethlehem, Pennsylvania, I vowed, "This will be the last time!" Once there, for whichever mother crisis or required holiday, I passed the time in the fabrication of meaning and connection. I made a pilgrimage to familiar settings, straining for Significance; I made my rounds, trying to manufacture evidence of belonging to my place and my family of origin. I would walk around the corridors of the beautifully preserved Moravian buildings where I'd gone to school; work up an enthusiasm for the triumph of history preserved; march around the behemoth of the defunct Bethlehem Steel plant; drive by the old paint mill, sunk in an oak-lined divot by the creek, that had stained its landscape a red that faded to pink over many years.

From the strain of trying to manufacture some connection, I'd cross over into numbness and then revert to my old hatred of the place. And so I began to call it Bethlehempennsylvania-all-one-word as a tribute to my loathing. Bethlehempenn-sylvania, with its population of the pale and the corpulent; its cultural signature of bovine sensibility and bemused con-formity; its emasculated river; its humidity that prevailed from May through October, enhancing the lassitude and feeling of entrapment; its foul air that invited polyps of all kinds and sizes—any mucous membrane was up for grabs. All this and more was crammed into the linked noun "Bethlehempenn-sylvania." The loathing was genuine, seeded by my fear of getting stuck forever.

I'd return to my actual home, in Seattle, tremendously relieved and ready to reconstitute my Self. A month would pass before, like clockwork, Mother's call would arrive: "Sweetie, sweetie, come home!" It felt like a really sad and grown-up version of the Lucy–Charlie Brown football moment. You know the one. It is autumn. Fall sports mania blares. Lucy promises Charlie Brown that this time, *for real*, she will hold the football steady as he approaches for his kick. She does not. Again and again, he is wary; he succumbs; too late, he kicks the empty air. Bethlehempennsylvania was my Charlie Brown football moment.

No sooner would I accomplish my "last" visit, having wrung every squeeze of Significance from the place and the parents and the tasks at hand, than it would start all over. What had been accomplished? Would I ever get to leave the place? Was this odd recidivism proof that I had not yet mastered the important tasks of adulthood? Bethlehempennsylvania was the weariness of self-effacement, every example in my life of not being seen. Linking the words made that place into a being—a character upon whose head and shoulders anguish might be pommeled.

Of course, it being *my* origin, delight was etched there, too —the contours of the fields, peculiar to eastern Pennsylvania; the wonderful variety of deciduous trees; the brittle, wispy vegetation along the creek. But the Stout realm and the gifts of nature did not customarily mix. So Bethlehempennsylvania remained a curse. It flayed. It persisted. I created my antidote with this flick of language.

SEVEN

⇌

Alice

POLLY AND HELEN HAD NOT PERFORMED AS GATEWAYS
toward happy aging, and I tossed them from me like autumn
leaves. My intentions for working with the elderly had seemed
twofold—to understand something about aging and by extension to prepare myself for it, and to seek work that would
inspire me to practice loving-kindness. Tossing is not an end
toward either, and Alice, my newest, would only strengthen my
urge to flee.

Eighty-two, displaced, and bitter, Alice kept herself alive
by complaining. In a constant twit about some meanness or
stupidity obtruding on a universe better managed, in her view,
by Isaac Newton, she wanted more than anything else to be
heard. Each week, our precious four hours filled with a
recitation of miseries, demonstrating an astonishing capacity
for her renewed surprise at the same microscopic ills.

My job was to take her out to lunch, but what she really
wanted was a place to sit and smoke while complaining. She

chain-smoked. This was a problem. Smoking is not permitted in most Seattle restaurants. That left Denny's, a palace of mediocrity, where every item on the menu is dipped, breaded, or fried, producing in the diner flatulence, fat, and eventually heart disease. For Alice, however, the dining experience was secondary to her smoking. As soon as she was seated, she'd retrieve the pack of Carltons from her purse, draw the ashtray to her even before she looked at the menu, light up, inhaling the smoke as if it were attached to a life-giving straw, and ask, "Do you mind?"

Every Wednesday at noon, Alice would be waiting in the parking lot of the Queen Anne Manor, a tiny, dry, old, puffing thing. A mauve raincoat, badly fitting and stained, and a plastic rain bonnet protected her from the outdoors, even when no rain threatened. She always clutched an umbrella and a gray-beige purse. I would leap out of the driver's seat and jog to her side. When asked, "How are you?" I would make sure to paint a pretty picture, pointing out such features of the day as sunshine, the autumn flowers still in bloom, and gratitude, or, if it were raining, I'd beam and say, "How cozy to be in a warm car."

Then I'd ask, "How are *you?*" and hope she'd take this as her cue to begin a sunny little list of her own. Instead, a rant would follow. Delivering her tirades, she'd duck and bob, as if trying to pump enough air to sustain the labors of breathing, complaining, and keeping her head erect. Her raspy, wheezy voice, forced up and out of her throat, made me think that she had emphysema.

And here I must confess what really bugged me—and that this numbingly trivial fact bugged me, bugged me even more: *Alice was not cute.* Honestly, the flight of cute alarmed me. I feared its flight from me. I had patched over countless imperfections of my own with ingratiating cuteness.

I thought of the time I lived on Lopez, one of the San Juan Islands in Puget Sound, with my newly minted love. We had strung a clothesline between the hemlock and the willow tree. The clothesline was, in fact, a highlight of country life, for there is nothing quite so sweet as clean laundry fluttering in the breeze. However, one thing began to sully this great pleasure. My newly minted love had a tendency to grab the wet clothes in fistfuls and wad them on the line. You know how wet blobs of toilet paper look when they've been lobbed against a wall? That's how the line looked when she "hung up" our clothes to dry. The small items—socks, underpants, cotton jerseys—appeared on the clothesline like TP wads. It took these wads *days* to dry. I failed to understand why my love, no longer newly minted, refused to make the connection between hanging laundry on the line in a way that maximized the surface area and the laundry's actually drying. As it happened, the bunched little items did not begin to dry until I rearranged them.

In the beginning, I did this happily, but then I grew resentful. And, as often happens with resentment, it expressed itself as self-righteous incredulity. *How could she be so . . . stupid?* Was it her upbringing? Was hers a family-of-origin chagrin? What was her problem? Is it not something that all who do the laundry know instinctively—that balled-up, wet clothes do not dry if you leave them in moist wads? It drove me wild. After a year of unproductive wondering, I ceased to find her cute at all.

This particular flight of cute suggested that for all of us, it is only a matter of time.

And then there was the flight of the appropriate. After all, to be so old and so in bondage to smoking flew in the face of my belief that age brings to the recipient restraint and wisdom. Alice seemed determined to do herself in with rancor, chagrin, and cigarettes. When she wanted a change from Denny's, smoking drove the choice. Thus, from time to time, we'd find ourselves in dark, creepy places—sports bars, in which the *clack* of cutlery on china and the *click* of pool balls and cues, and the bank of liquor bottles lit up like showgirls, collided with the incessant roar of an overhead TV. Or we'd be shown into the windowless back rooms of diners, where the menus featured applesauce and sauerkraut under the vegetable heading. Always a TV blared, and some screeching team sport intercut with advertisements for SUVs, both promulgating aggressive, chrome-infected happiness. I would leave our dates bleary-eyed, swearing I'd had lunch with someone who had close ties with the underworld, however benign Alice might appear, and I would be humming that rueful song sung by Peggy Lee—"Is that all there is?" I would sing the bits that I remembered, barely conscious of doing so, and then I would catch myself answering the question: "Yes—why, yes, it is." Alice was living proof that this was so.

After six months, I couldn't take Alice anymore, but I am the sort of person who endures spasms of guilt when I have to bid even the cat farewell for a couple of hours. I'm no good thinking I've let someone down, even if just Kitty, so I knew I'd put off telling Alice until the last five minutes of our final day.

Nevertheless, that morning, I performed my rituals with care. Quitting Alice would be no hit-and-run affair but rather a decision as well thought out and kindly executed as possible.

I opened my morning's spiritual reading matter: Pema Chodron's *When Things Fall Apart*:

Hopelessness means that we no longer have the spirit for holding our trip together. We may still want to hold our trip together. We long to have some reliable, comfortable ground under our feet, but we've tried a thousand ways to hide and a thousand ways to tie up all the loose ends, and the ground just keeps moving under us. *Trying to get lasting security teaches us a lot, because if we never try to do it, we never notice that it can't be done* [emphasis mine].

Maybe Alice was ahead of the game and her genuine grumpiness and refreshingly consistent outlook held the spiritual key. But what about happiness? What about joy? Surely, if one has mastered the task of seeing things clearly, as they truly are, a kind of joyful acceptance might follow?

SHE WAS STANDING IN THE PARKING LOT, HER TINY SELF pointed toward Ballard, and when she got into the car, she announced that she wanted to go shopping.

"What would you like to shop for, Alice?" I asked, pretending that her every wish was my command.

"Oh, we'll just go," she said in her soft, shallow little pant. "That's *real* shopping. If you already know what you want when you go shopping, that's an errand, not *real* shopping at all."

As usual, she puffed through lunch—ate, and puffed, and extinguished, and lit up, and puffed some more—all the while asking, "Do you mind?"

My low mood shifted into something worse. The cumulative effect of working for, or with, "my" old people—Helen and Polly, and with Mother adding her special ingredient to the mix—tipped me into anger. I was being appropriated to align with brittle views. I realized that my resentment at being hauled back to Bethlehempennsylvania had this flavor. Called to collude with a view I found untrue, I earned Mother's love through self-betrayal.

Alice blew her smoke over her hamburger and my eggs, so bent upon her puffing that even her self-congratulatory reminiscences were sullied with these exhalations. My intent to explore aging and realize death by sitting at the feet of the aged had been derailed. I was furious. They had been absolutely no help whatsoever.

"My mother's very sick," I said to Alice, puffing her way through a piece of mud pie the size of her purse. "I have to go back East to help her."

I had promised to bring her a map of Ohio, her native state, about which we'd had an occasionally merry conversation. For some reason that my still-fit, fifty-ish-year-old brain could not comprehend, Alice found it impossible to get one. So I had torn Ohio from my Rand-McNally road atlas, pretty sure that I would never toodle through this state again, and this was the offering that I slid toward her. It was the least, on this sorry day, that I could do, the one request that I could actually honor. Of course, Ohio preceded North Dakota, the loss of which I grieved, as one never knew—I might, after this seminar with "my" old people, get a hankering to go spend time in the badlands.

And that was it. That was how I ended it, with a perfunctory "I'm sorry" and no auxiliary explanation. I knew I was the highlight of her week. I knew that what we had was, in Alice's mind, both friendship and rapport. Her face fell, of course. A few urgent grunts sounded underneath her panting. Her pale eyes, magnified behind enormous glasses, didn't try to conceal her disappointment. Something else emerged from her gaze, a desperate knowledge that *here* was where she'd gotten to—uprooted and repotted in a strange and friendless place, stripped of powers, bereft of meaningful exchanges, no glowing satisfaction of a life well lived, no swelling chords of spiritual attainment, just pellets of complaints thrown into the wind.

⇌

Commentary:

METTA

METTA, OR LOVING-KINDNESS MEDITATION, REMAINS among the more arduous aspects of my Buddhist practice. One sits on the cushion and, through a progression of steps, invites the mind to surrender to the heart. One might repeat these phrases—*may I be happy; may I be free from suffering; may I live peacefully; may I be happy*—and extend, subsequently, the benediction to a dear friend, then to an enemy, then to a perfect stranger. Nothing short of radiating the roils and waves of love out into the needful world must follow.

Loving-kindness graced neither my time with nor my words about poor Alice. I occupied a horrified despair with her, and this prevented me from telling you some facts that would make her character more sympathetic. Alice was originally from Ohio and never tired of informing me it was the Buckeye State. She'd been a chemist and, when she proved willing to be cajoled out of peevishness, revealed odd and fascinating memories of her professional life, particularly during World War II. I was always surprised when Alice set aside her ill will and, warming to her memories, revealed intelligence, curiosity, and a wicked sense of humor.

She remembered, for example, when detergent was first formulated, and so the first wave, so to speak, set off a sudsing catastrophe in one of the Great Lakes, lasting weeks. She could toss off the names of chemicals and compounds the way others could the common names of plants—"short-chain alkyl naphthalene sulfonates"—tapping the ash against a Denny's Bakelite ashtray. She could intersperse amusing recollections of the übersudsing debacle in the Great Lakes with chemical theory: "It would have been in 1946 that there was a breakthrough in formulation and an all-purpose laundry detergent came on the scene. It was a surfactant-builder combination that made it possible. That's the basic cleaning ingredient, you understand." And I'd nod, impressed and mildly saddened that she could not carry into the present her sense of engagement, her being of use.

Alice had been stationed in many chemical factories in the Midwest during the war. Her delight as she reminisced about her work—the outfits endured, the detox procedures, the labs —indicated that she had felt herself to be a part of something larger.

Alice also had a daughter, with whom she seemed locked in resentment. Alice had raised her as a single mother, because of a divorce. I didn't know that people actually did that in the

1940s—oh, there were the old films and such, but the dissolution of marriage was thought to be so lurid. The Stouts had never had divorced friends or acquaintances. I'd had a good friend in high school whose mother was divorced, and my parents regarded this girl as risqué, fast, and sexually precocious. It did not help that she looked like Natalie Wood. In fact, before graduation, Nora did run off with Mr. Betzler, our overweight, Cro-Magnon-browed gym teacher, when she was a voluptuous eighteen. Alice's divorce implied rich underpinnings, but nothing more about this would be revealed.

In any event, it was her daughter who had urged Alice to leave Ohio and make the move to Queen Anne Manor. She reported this, repeatedly, with great resentment, a tone magnified in her contempt for the demented residents, the staff, the food, the stupid rules. She was unpleasant. She complained. Her world had shriveled.

I felt sorry for Alice, although I did not like her. My choices seemed to be to collude with her, agreeing that everything sucked, or, grimly, put on a happy face. Alice ran counter to my happy belief that old age brings the gifts of self-acceptance, completion, and gratitude.

And so my intent to sit in some bright, raw awareness of aging, to seek guides through the fearsome mysteries of dying, had met thus far with dismal un-success. I had learned, instead, that one must watch out for the crossroads where complaining meets the flight of cute and, sensing the approach, establish healthy routines and a happy outlook. I just could not embrace my inner Alice. Her predicament unnerved me and, it seemed, caught even her off guard. What if you live a good life and it dead-ends in a strange town, in a tiny room, with miseries for friendship? How would you rehearse for that?

In our little Stout unit, *not* complaining was a virtue positioned somewhere between churchgoing and being very, very clean. Its suppression commanded the respect due such achievements as the deft execution of Chopin's études or the crippling perseverance of the bonsai artist. I had hoped that spending time in the company of Alice, who complained with verve and vigor, might prove tonic and amusing. I was wrong. My experience with her demonstrated instead, as Anthony Lane wrote when describing the films of Preston Sturges, "the . . . radical possibility that age makes us not sadder but more comic—brimming with the sour yeast of a silly world."

EIGHT

⇌

John

"YOU'RE GOING TO LOVE THIS MAN," HARRIET SAID, reading me the work order over the phone. Alice dispensed with, and the most recent Bethlehempennsylvania sortie survived, it was time to get to work.

"John McDermott, eighty-six, a widower of nine years," Harriet read, "wants companion services. Retired professor of classics, losing short-term memory. He's a writer, working on an article. Encourage him to write." There was a worrisome aside: "Has anxiety about his condition."

"What's wrong with him?" I asked.

"Dementia. He's got dementia," Harriet said, in a way that made it sound rather gay. "He fades in and out—short-term-memory loss. But he is your professor!" she continued, as if handing me the world. "His daughters say that he adores Italy and everything Italian. He lived in Rome. He is," she concluded, "a treasure."

"And I am supposed to . . . ?" I prodded.

I heard Harriet rustle the work order. She said, "Take him shopping."

Now, I am not one to feel calm, restored, or creative in that medium. I mean, grocery shopping, yes. Flowers—point me in the direction. But shopping as a genre, an activity? As creative as I get is my yearly jaunt to Office Depot, hunting legal pads and stalking the latest in ballpoint pens and brightly colored variations on your basic desk equipment. So I asked with some concern, "What kind of shopping?"

Harriet sighed. "It says here," she said, "that he loves Costco."

I hung up, eager to continue my adventure, the newest episode, with an ancient philosopher and meaningful consumer moments. I figured that John's dementia would only add dimension. After all, weren't now-and-again slides into dementia similar to my greased-pole moments? One's hold on a self seemed no firmer than that.

HARRIET HAD WARNED ME ABOUT THE WORRISOME PAUSE that would follow my knock on the door of an *old person*. "Hold steady," she advised. I realized, sadly, that this tip constituted my training. If there was a doorbell, I was told to ring at three-minute intervals; if not, to knock repeatedly and wait. And so I knocked at John's front door. I waited and I leaned. I waited, studying the terra cotta tiles of the front porch, fearing an encounter between them and John's eighty-six-year-old hips. I rang the bell again. I waited, shifting my weight, and rattled the small brass latch on the screen door. I restrained myself from bolting, pounding on a neighbor's door, and calling 911.

It was a pretty part of town, and his a neighborhood of

stately homes that bordered a small park. Turning right at the end of his block, you'd teeter on a sickening pitch of hill to be greeted by this view: the Cascades, snowcapped in the distance; in the near, Lake Washington and Portage Bay, the cut joining it to Lake Union, on which bobbed a pretty string of houseboats, festooned with hanging pots of ferns and flowers. And with the peripheral slice of the University of Washington in view, this street designated John's place in the world, secured in 1948, when he moved to Seattle, adventurous wife and three children eager and in tow. This was his street, and even in November, which in Seattle makes us pale and dispirited, it banished gloom.

Finally, with a series of tugs and jerks, the door opened, and there stood a once-tall man wearing a misshapen tweed blazer over a red and blue–striped rugby shirt, and serviceable khakis. His feet collapsed into listing oxfords. His feathery white hair curled at the back of his neck, and his face reflected a chiseled elegance.

"Thank you," he said boomingly, opening the door wider, and took my hand. Harriet had provided some familial history. John's two daughters were engaged in a struggle to persuade their father to sell the big house and move him into an assisted-living facility. Zealously, he rejected their pleas and discounted their concerns with such strategies as forgetting, raging haughtily, and medicating the indignity with tumblers of cheap white wine.

Alert, thus, to the possibility of these little dents and fissures in his composure, I followed him into the living room. Dark green walls and drawn curtains running from floor to ceiling drove daylight from the room. There was an odor of smoldering pipe. He took a seat in an improvised corner between the French doors of the living room and the end of a long sofa, covered with a dusty pink sheet. His chair, with its erect back and narrow seat pan, was, like Helen's, not designed for comfort. Nevertheless, this incongruous corner seemed his customary place. He squeezed between the chair and an aluminum tray table upon which lay scattered pens and pencils, bits of newspaper, a *TV Guide*, clipped and tattered coupons, and a pile of paper clips. The trill of a canary startled the drowsy, cluttered room.

"What would you like to do?" I asked, my voice jarring in the gloom.

"Do?" he asked. His brow furrowed. "Ah, well, what should I *do* with you?"

This made me nervous. "We need to make a plan," I said. Frantically, he began to look from side to side, as if caught unprepared in the role of host with neither wife nor tea tray at the ready. John's was a stranded husband's look, augmented by a horrified expression indicating he had forgotten who I was.

My training had not talked about this moment. My training had not instilled in me the confidence of coping. Together, we fell into a sad, gray-brown mush, where form and structure were abandoned. I could feel him make fluttering hand motions in his mind, shooing me away so that he could nurse his wonderment in private.

"I'm here to help," I said, not feeling helpful at all.

"No, no, no, I don't need help," he said, with offended dignity.

I was tempted to rejoin, "Yes, yes, yes, you do," but how could I presume? That is, how could I press my judgment into the sturdy wall of his denial? He'd been a professor—of the *classics*, no less.

"Is there laundry to fold?" I asked, thinking some household activity might right our fragile craft.

He looked at me in further horror. "Oh, *the woman* does that," he said. He'd gotten it in his mind that I was above menial work. I took him at his word that there was, indeed, such a one, *the woman*, imagining a stout char, lumpen of feature, pink of face, square of build—something like Mr. Toad on his barge—playing washerwoman.

He was embarrassed, clearly, to imagine me privy to his soiled shirts and underwear, so I didn't insist. The trouble was, he was treating me more like a visiting dignitary than like hired help. He seemed to want no help, or at least to have forgotten that someone in his family had hired me to help, and what sort of help, when *the woman* did the cleaning and the dusting and the tidying, although, looking about, I wondered if *the woman* herself might be one of Helen's Bulgarians.

Despairing of being useful, I thought of literature and rallied. Perhaps I could read to him. Perhaps we could discuss writing, something I knew about, and philosophy, something that everybody had. Plus, Harriet had suggested that I might encourage him to finish an essay that she believed him to be writing.

"Harriet tells me you're working on an essay," I began.

"Yes, yes," he boomed, and his countenance brightened. "An essay. Do you write?"

I confessed that, yes, I did, and we were on track again. "What do you write?" he asked.

"I am writing a novel," I said modestly.

"Oh." He brought his hands together as if I'd given him a beautifully wrapped present to be savored.

"But sometimes," I cautioned hastily, "talking about it

when it's in the very beginning stages, well . . . can sort of dent the initiative," I said. *Dent the initiative?*

"Tell me about your essay," I began again. "Can I, maybe, help you with the typing?" The task, and its simplicity, might prove soothing.

"Ah, yes, yes, that would be tremendously helpful. But first I, first I . . ."

"First you, first you . . ." I paddled my hands in front of my chest to stir memory, but his sentence collapsed. His face followed. Our bright moment had dulled into a fatigue of tracking. I leaned forward. "First you must . . . organize your notes?" I ventured.

"Yes, that's it exactly," he said, with palpable relief. "And now I would like to show you my study."

We pulled our way, teetering, up the staircase—he unsteady and frail, I following at a pace that made it hard to keep my balance. His essay, he explained, concerned a philosopher of ancient Greece whose name began with an "E." Even as John said it, I couldn't keep the name in mind, because my encounter with the Greeks amounted to my having been ill cast, in college, as a chorus member in Sophocles's *Electra*, and also to having taken Philosophy 101.

Both of these regrettable confrontations took place at Lake Erie College for Women in 1967. Craig Stark was the college's single philosophy professor, a wiry-haired redhead who so totally looked the part that in his classroom I would always think I was in my acting class, and thus could never wrap my mind around the gravity of the topics at hand. Philosophy as a course of study seemed about as useful as fine arts, where I got stuck in my sophomore year, never to prove myself more capable of becoming a productive member of society by expressing an interest in and aptitude for, say, Spanish or economics or even anthropology, where, in a pinch, you could get to teach at a liberal arts college somewhere and be a brainy lesbian with a mandate to cultivate voyeurism built right into your career.

What I never understood then, as now, was why men—at least, *mostly* it was men—sat around dreaming up convoluted thought processes and mind-numbing abstractions. Fortunately, I had my background in Christian Science, so I knew the highways and byways of thinking that was not well thought out. In spite of this early training, though, philosophy gave me a headache. I mean, wasn't the point of studying philosophy to help you figure out the meaning of life? The closest I had ever come to experiencing a meaning-of-life moment was while reading Jean-Paul Sartre's *Nausea* when I was sixteen. Now, *that* made terrific sense, and seemed an excellent text to prepare a young person for the perils ahead.

John's early Greek philosopher whose name started with an "E" was known for a radical theory that had something to do with fire in the human eye. But as John explained it, the fire in his own eye flickered. The thought fled, and with it the automatic linking of sentences to sense and to each other. Whenever John tried to launch a train of thought, the train derailed and the contents of his mental cargo spilled like little puffs of lint from his trouser pocket, and then in silence we would drop our eyes, as if the puffs could be retrieved, and look sternly at the floor. They were gone, though. Gone, gone.

"Gone," we would say to each other, and over time it would serve as code.

Small, blue, cloth-bound notebooks ran the length of an eight-foot shelf over an equal length of desk, a sturdy vessel in which to weather the tempests of argument and thought. His notebooks held forty years of scholarly endeavor—commentaries, arguments, collegial quibbles, and rants—all of it handwritten. A talus of paper clips and rubber bands and India-rubber erasers and university-issued pencils reduced to stubs littered the desk. Behind it, on a shelf, a glass humidor housed a fabulously aromatic pipe tobacco that released whiffs of cherry and smoky tea. It was a study whose mess contributed to the cozy atmosphere, but it was a graveyard, too. Archaic debris on a desk that had itself grown dusty, and the brittle notebooks, untouched for many years, made it clear that engagement and vitality had fled long ago.

And so our tour of the study threw the status of John's essay into perspective. It had not been touched for years and would remain so. For us there would be no learned project, no bonding based, as I had hoped, on the life of the mind. Or at least the life of the mind as I was accustomed to defining it.

We returned to the living room to gather our wits in the cramped Dim Corner. In the dull wattage of John's diminished powers, my mind grew torporous, falling like the living room curtains that hung in decrepit angles of neglect. But how much of my palpable despair depended on the rigid value that I placed on work, "meaningful" work, with its proof that the self is worthy? The question grew thorns. If, when old, one became incapable even of reflecting on one's life's work, what could the notebooks and dusty study be but a daily stab and sorrow? And was the world less rich in the absence of John's essay on his ancient Greek philosopher? What if making good soup and taking care of the canary and accepting the truth of the melting, shifting self were, in the end, as important as the sustained rank among peers and the sunshine of published writing?

Our time was up. We roused ourselves, agreeing to meet weekly. How, in our arrangement, I wondered, would we avoid despair? If, over time, the Dim Corner were to prove our meeting place, my real job would be not to flinch, not to flee our gazing. Ever the host, John helped me into my coat. In the hall, boxes and broken appliances clustered against a gigantic grandfather clock. Mentioning that my father collected clocks and had a specimen like this of his own, I asked him if it worked.

"Oh, yes," he said, mysteriously saying no more.

"Well?" I prompted.

He looked at me as if I should know better. "I've stopped the mechanism," he said. "I cannot stand to be reminded of time's passing."

NINE

⇌

The Quandaried Self

EVERY WEDNESDAY WE'D START OVER. HE ANSWERED MY knock with a hearty "thank you," prematurely delighted with our visit. He took my arm, leading me into the living room to review his precious objects. We paid homage to the carved heads that had originally belonged to distinguished professors who had visited many years ago. His wife, Mary, had been a sculptor, and I think we made these ritual rounds to reconnect him to memory. Then we'd arrive back at the chair in the Dim Corner and sitting would commence, whereupon he'd ask, "What shall I do with you today?"

Out of genuine interest, I'd begin to ask him questions. Obligingly, he'd fish for a detail. It would nibble the edges of his brain, and he'd reel it in, his hands patting the air to give the memory shape. He grasped a name—Ted Roethke, teaching at the University of Washington at the same time—but then his eyes would rake the space before him as he lost both the sense and the thread of his story, and the name, Roethke, would plummet like an elevator's descent to the ground floor, and his face would fall slack. My own sense of time and space came untethered. John's memories behaved like irritating guests who strode in and out of mind as if through a loose-hinged door. I began feeling like Cordelia to his King Lear.

Sir, do you know me? I would be tempted, like Cordelia, to ask.

I imagined him replying, *Pray, do not mock me: I am a very foolish fond old man, fourscore and upward, not an hour more nor less; and, to deal plainly, I fear I am not in my perfect mind. Methinks I should know you. . . .*

So, once the narrative stalled and the syntax drifted, over time it was silence that issued from the Dim Corner, and we'd drop into a deeper realm of the sustained and vibrant gaze. The house might creak, the canary trill, an afternoon stab of sunlight penetrate the gloom, a car approach and pass softly as we sat finding solace and mystery in the gaze. It was all I could do to hold steady. Unburdened by the need to sustain the architecture of a self, we were free to drift in the realm of pure sensation.

Panicked about having to actually hang out in the flesh with my literary allusions—Shakespeare's fools and madmen; Samuel Beckett's disenfranchised ranters—I called Harriet, who with a heavy sigh reminded me that I was the one here with the intact identity, and thus the one in charge. "*You're* the one who is competent," she said, as if telling me for the tenth time to wipe my feet and quit tracking up the carpet. "You've got to haul him out of the house," she said. "Didn't you read the service order? It says he loves to go to Costco, Goodwill, and Safeway."

"Well, I keep asking him if he needs anything from those places, and he keeps saying no," I said.

"You're there to determine what he needs," said Harriet, reeling me in with her social-worker voice, implying strain tempered by a little patience. "These people are confused. They have no idea what they want or how to structure their time. And," she added, "if you're freaking out, you and I will do lunch."

"Great," I said. "But before we *do* lunch, I have to tell you that I think he's drinking."

A sigh. A pause. "What makes you think that?" she asked.

"I smell it on his breath," I said. "Sometimes he's really disoriented when I get there. Like he's already eaten his lunch by ten in the morning. Like he's wobbly. I mean, more-than-usual wobbly."

"He has a problem with depression. Maybe I should call his daughter. Come to think of it, under the circumstances, why shouldn't he drink? At his age, given all that, wouldn't you?"

AFTER SOME COAXING, JOHN AGREED TO ACCOMPANY me on outings—to Safeway, Goodwill, Costco, Pacific Foods— and when I feared our brains would rot or his closets overflow with the surfeit of toilet paper, Kleenex, and paper towels, I would attempt field trips out in nature. I held a terrifically ambitious hope that someday we'd make it to the zoo. Over many months, a variety of adventures ensued, all characterized by a pace that strained credulity and by mania salted with despair.

⇌

We Prepare

I WOULD ARRIVE AT NOON. AFTER FIVE MINUTES, HE would have made it to the door.

"It took you long enough," he'd say, tugging the door open in fits and starts. Standing in the foyer, I would observe no light in the house, but for the TV's flicker. An eruption of nonsense might ensue.

"Do you want to cheat?" he might ask.

"Cheat at what?" I'd answer, trying to get my bearings.

"*Oui, oui,*" he'd reply, tossing his arms up.

"Do you want to go to Paris?" I'd rejoin, still struggling to understand.

"Ah, a beautiful language, French," he'd say.

"Do you speak French?" I'd ask, resigned to madness. The assortment of coupons and tattered lists, an ancient cookbook arguing for Scottish cuisine, keys and loose change littering the radiator, did not help.

"Oh, no, no, no, no, no," he'd trill. "Not even *un peu.*"

"Do you want to go to France, John?" I might ask, looking pointedly at my watch.

"No, I don't suppose we could do that," he'd say sadly, and then brighten. "But I could send you home. You could go home and get back to your writing." And he would smile again, and wink, and then I would smell the wine.

It was sweet and sour on his breath, and it made me frantic, as it was the main, recurring item on the grocery list— French Colombard, a nasty, cheap jug wine of uncertain and shady lineage. Every Wednesday, we had to buy a new, four-jug case of it, which we would add to the inventory almost entirely filling the narrow pantry.

And so we discussed the weather, whether coat and hat were needed. He'd poke in sundry pockets for a coupon book, a list. I'd open the door, and a holiday spirit would seize us. The air would be sniffed, the sky's behavior noted, the slippery stair negotiated, the soaked moss on the pavement circumvented. Lowering him into the car, I would put my hand on his head and cup his skull, endeared to the corn-silk texture of his pure white hair.

On Our Way

WE WOULD GAZE GRIMLY THROUGH THE WINDSHIELD at the traffic puddling on the terrible I-5. Swaddled in winter wraps, facing the undulate, fat coil of cars, we were relieved from the intensity of eye contact sustained from the Dim Corner, and it was in these moments that John would say, "I am losing my mind." I would steal a look at him, sitting stiffly beside me, his hands perched on his knees, his beret rakish. Enviously, I'd note that he had the sort of head designed for berets—a well-shaped skull; a hewn and aristocratic nose; a noble brow. My beret, perched like a rotting mushroom on my pea head, made me look dim-witted.

Since John was, indeed, losing his mind, my choices of reply fell either to deceitful, "There, theres" or to silence, acknowledging the awful truth of what he said. I could not, "There, there" him.

He seemed occasionally to know exactly what was happening to him. He seemed occasionally not to.

⇌

Recognition

A PEAR-SHAPED LITTLE MAN THWARTED OUR PROGRESS across the Safeway parking lot. A beret lay like a pancake dead center on top of his head. Unlike John's, his was not the sort of head designed for berets. The two old men stopped in the middle of the thoroughfare. They sniffed and blinked, trying to place each other. Something kindred was recognized. Their hands wobbled toward each other. They grasped and pumped. Their faces struck poses of wonder.

"Do I know you?" the small, plump man asked.

"I was a classics professor at the university," John announced.

"I speak Turkish, French, Russian," the man announced in kind, as if these details might tease out some recognition. He had an accent. It sounded Eastern European.

John paused, still smiling with bonhomie. "Do you speak"— he paused again, fishing in his mind for a comment that would provide continuity—"Norwegian?"

I did a double take. The pear-shaped man didn't find this strange. He merely declined knowledge of Norwegian.

"Keep busy," John cried. "I have been retired for fifteen years."

"Me," replied the pear, pointing fondly to his heart, "four."

"Yes, yes, it is necessary to stay busy," exhorted John.

"He needs exercise. You should take him running," the little man said sternly, his pudgy finger heading for my breast.

I tugged at John. We rallied and almost made it through the wide entrance of the Safeway, where John planted himself to look over the checkers. "Ah, there's Audrey," he said, lifting his hand at the bank of checkers, as shoppers and carts stacked up behind us.

Wherever we went, there was fragility and tottering, stopping in the middle of entryways, elliptical recollections, backed-up shopping carts and shoppers. Our shuffle, never steady, inevitably dwindled to an almost-lifting-in-place of feet. John seemed compelled to stop in the middle of busy intersections, absorbed in recollection or trying to track a thought. I worked up a feverish anxiety just standing with him, gazing across the unnavigable parking lot at our destination, trying to push our frail vessels out of the paths of oncoming cars and pedestrians in their normal hurry. I would hook his arm through mine and shove him gently, like a tugboat. Firmly, but with a note of desperation, I would say, "Please, John, don't stop now."

The Itinerary

IN THE DRUGSTORE, WE MIGHT STAND BEFORE THE display of ginkgo biloba. He would scratch his head and say, "I need this for my memory," and I would say, "You bought two jars last week," and he would widen his eyes in horror and cover, with fluttering hand, his astonished mouth, and then laugh. Every Wednesday, he would say, "I'd like to show you my drugstore itinerary," as if we had arrived in Rome, about to pore over our wish lists and walking maps for the day. We pushed an empty shopping cart around monumental cubes of featured items—light bulbs, seasonal candies, vitamins, hand soaps, dry-roast, no-salt peanuts, jam. Mostly the cart stayed empty, yet it seemed crucial to our meandering promenade. People dispensed kind smiles as I worked to point the cart away from the vulnerable displays. Everyone else in the drugstore was possessed of focus and functioning lists and full carts, steered by the commonly held view of time. For us, time was air and water. As we parted the stream of shoppers, people gazed at us because we were adrift, alighting briefly on some needful thing. It was quite convivial in its way, for when one is relieved of the burden of tasks, what is left but the yearning to dip one's weary self into the human current?

We wove and peered and reminisced. We might have been adrift, but we were not deluded. When he said the awful, scary things, about which one can do nothing, neither of us flinched or looked away. I did not placate. He did not dissemble. The moment would descend like a flurry of dry leaves. We would pause inside the rustle. Then I would draw his attention to the Kleenex on sale, or farther afield to some detail of human oddity, or even farther afield to something outside—a blazing elm, because beauty walks arm in arm with sorrow. The thing of it was, John's heart could still be dazzled.

The Goodwill

IN THE GOODWILL, IT WAS A POT LID HE WAS AFTER. A colorful assortment of people were pawing through acres of clothing racks; myriad nationalities and languages competed for the goods. Exotic headgear loomed over the racks, drained otherwise of color by the overhead fluorescent lights. I felt as if I were in the aviary at the zoo—flashes of exotic wings and head coverings. We shuffled. John leaned heavily on his shopping cart. Burt Bacharach's "I Say a Little Prayer" was piped gaily through the air, saturated with particles of history from the fibers of used clothing, and the fact of no windows, and old footwear and headwear and bed wear and underwear. The Bacharach penetrated this grainy, unwashed air with its saccharine vows, as if love, with its flypaper reach—the brief relief of it, the pouty disappointments—was the only thing that mattered.

Slowly we shuffled past bins of disemboweled appliances, past a monumental case displaying a stuffed grizzly bear, past rows of broken furniture, past the teeming bins of destitute and tangled stuffed toys, to arrive at housewares. Intrigued by the aisles of pots and pans, John would search wonderingly for lids. The problem was that the exact pot—its size and the purpose for which a lid was needed—could not be brought to mind. And so, after fingering many lids, he would give a long, sad sigh and declare the search to be of no use whatsoever. We would start the long trek back. He would never spend more than a dollar.

THOSE WERE OUR ADVENTURES. WE WOULD RETURN laden with the same treasures every week, and the naughty jugs of wine. The job was proving too ambitious—to snuggle up to the phenomenon of aging, cup its bony shoulders in my palms, let it lean against my hip and bosom; to sniff and grip and fondle. That my experiment with "my" old people had evolved into a study of identity, and assaults upon it, brought small comfort. Here was John's, slipping off him like an old mask whose elastic strap had rotted.

The self was revealed dependent on a series of assumptions—the easy getting out of bed in the morning; the finding of one's socks; the smooth descent downstairs to sit in front of morning coffee and buttered toast, prepared by one's mate. Now there is no mate, no fragrant coffee, waiting toast. Such defined the self as he and we might have known it. When the capabilities fragment, and the socks hide, and the staircase threatens, and the love departs—the self, his and mine . . . well, this was my question. The belief that the self is fixed and solid spells danger and sorrow in the end.

"DO YOU TAKE A DRINK BEFORE LUNCH?" ASKED JOHN as we shuffled past the lounge on our way upstairs to the faculty club for a long-anticipated date. His fond glance into the vaulted, gloomy room suggested that a drink, or even several, *before* lunch might, in his young and valiant years, indeed have passed for lunch itself.

For weeks, I had ignored the invitation, doubting its legitimacy. After all, John typically eschewed any activity I suggested that didn't involve toilet paper acquisition or French Colombard. I did not think him capable of initiating such a normal, grown-up pleasantry as lunch. Nor had it occurred to me that he'd maintained an association with the university, however tangential. Had his invitation not issued from a time warp? And besides, I am not one to take a drink before or even with my lunch. Hauling John around sober was challenge enough. I called Margaret, his oldest daughter, my age, as I often did when John presented me with peculiar requests or mysterious claims.

"Oh, he's been talking about it with me for weeks," she said. "It's true—he does still go. It would thrill him if you would let him take you to lunch."

And so, fine, I agreed to go.

⇌

WE TOTTERED PAST THE LOUNGE, AND HE ASKED AGAIN, "Do you take a drink before lunch?" Seduction shimmered in the question. It seemed so naughty, so glamorous, so why-in-the-world-*not*? That seemed the sentiment behind his giggle. But his "drink before lunch" summoned the image of his pantry filled with cases of the terrible French Colombard. He became a different man—one testier and more confused—when drinking. It inspired me not to want to be a drunk at eighty. Call me superficial, but I knew that geriatric tippling would not help keep me cute. As I disclosed in my prickly bond with Alice, the flight of cute alarms me.

UNAWARE OF THE BLOCKAGE WE CREATED, JOHN TOOK tiny, sideways steps in the cafeteria line, leaning into the bank of daily specials. He peered, questioned, pondered, finally settling on the smallest possible serving of barley soup. I grabbed a handful of packaged crackers to keep the bowl company on its vast tray. He studied the dining room beyond the line, abuzz with collegial engagement, completely unaware that he was a fossil.

The world John once inhabited flinched when he approached, averted its eyes, or muttered falsities and platitudes. The world was ashamed, or it could not bear to meet the old man on his terms, which offended the belief in a forever-intact and well-assembled self. Here was the specter heralding everybody's future.

Finally we arrived at a table, and then came his labored descent into the chair, the parking of the cane against the table, its predictable fall and naughty clatter. He again studied the room, of more interest than his food. Even among the older professors, their white shirts disheveled, their bow ties knocked at sloppy angles, John looked ancient.

This would prove the cadence of our luncheon days: setting out in high spirits; met at the club by the dismissive wave of its director; the ordering of his frugal soup and my acidic salad; fatuities, placations, flinching, and pitying glances; the arrival at table, there briefly to rest; and then the wash of awareness denting and dimming our spirits. His eyes would make their tour around the big, bright room and blink, as if awakening. His jaw would drop as he searched the room for someone, anyone, whom he could call colleague and companion. Invariably, he'd alight upon Professor Macaw, with whom a ritual dialogue would follow—his reiteration, to me, of Macaw's victory over some departmental insurrection thirty years ago; Macaw's kindness as he chatted, treating this as *new* news; the fire in John's eye, recalling the incident as if it were yesterday's foment. Whatever bitterness lingered over that was magnified by the slight John nursed when the university had denied him an office, which he felt due him as a classics professor emeritus.

Macaw would return to his cronies. Intently John would watch him turn and go, and whatever vitality had stirred him in the small exchange would depart with Macaw. He would regard his tray with sorrow and feel himself to be out of the current, dipping back once a week only to be reminded that this was not his river.

IT WAS THUS WITH INCREDULITY AND NO SMALL AMOUNT of awe that I received the news that our lunches, in his mind, were all a great success.

"Shall we do it again?" he asked from his chair in the Dim Corner. Inspired, perhaps, by the triumph of our latest outing, he rose and took my hands in his. "Oh, yes," he said warmly. "Next week, we will go again."

I went to the kitchen to put away the groceries. Moments later, I heard the sound of water. I peeked into the dining room, and there stood John before his tall, once-elegant Norfolk Island pine, watering. Houseplant maintenance had not, thus far, proven his forte. Along the outer edge of a threadbare Persian carpet lived half a dozen plants, each one gasping for breath in its stately urn. It was a grim detail I had chosen to ignore, because it would have taken a horticultural wizard to convince the plants that their lives were worth saving. I saw that in his vigorous endeavor to water the plants, John's aim had not been good. Beside each plant spread a puddle, making for the rug. He looked up from his task and beamed. It was hard to find the heart to stop him.

"Um," I said, approaching slowly. He looked so happily involved in what clearly appeared a good houseplant deed.

"Um," I said again, "you're watering the floor."

He looked down at the stream of water and up at me, horror widening his features. I shooed him back to the corner and mopped up. I held out no hope for the poor plants' futures. Already fatal legginess and leaf drop prevailed, and that characterized the healthy population. Those beyond help, like the pine, were uniformly crisp, with a little tinge reminiscent of green. I expected that John would be in his Dim Corner, actively waiting for me to leave, so he could nap, or drink—whatever. The botched watering foreshadowed disaster. Who would clean up *this* mess, if not I, and bigger ones to follow?

So, yes, I said, we'd go to lunch the following Wednesday.

I told him that I'd call to remind him, because likely he'd forget. I said, "Don't eat lunch before we go to lunch," winking sternly. I intended the wink as a caution against morning consumption of the terrible French Colombard.

And then, Reader, I kissed him. I planted a kiss on the proffered cheek. It was the spontaneous projection of my fondness. He was plucky and sad and endearing and the closest I would ever come to experiencing the world of Samuel Beckett.

It *was* spontaneous, heartfelt. *Thank you; it was a lovely day*, it said, meaning that not precisely but rather as an acknowledgment of his recoveries from each humiliation that pocked our days. He would manage to pick himself up from the heap of disappointments and horrors to start over, with renewed delusion, and a sweetness in his heart that pulled him toward affection and delight.

Halfway through the moment, I recovered my mind. It was a mistake, I knew it. I finished up the kiss anyway.

He returned the cheek kiss, and the reserve that had contained our fondness for each other shifted. Would he now think he was my lover? Would the kiss shoo us into awkward, intimate collisions? Would he mistake me for his wife? I drew back, reaching for the safety of our old politeness. But no—a little candle in his eye told me that I was going to become a fixation.

I let myself out, got in the car, and drove to Fred Meyer. I needed some menstrual supplies. I was rather proud of still needing them at all, as I was somewhat over fifty. I did think it wickedly unfair to have to bleed while suffering my life-altering hot flashes. In a way, I didn't mind still bleeding. As long as I bled, I could believe myself still firmly in the ranks of the vital. Thus, I couldn't help observing, in the feminine-hygiene aisle, that my brand of tampons was on sale—Kotex regular absorbency, one hundred for $10. *"One hundred,"* I whispered, the need for an unknown actual amount commingling with greed. And this thought followed: this, indeed, could be my last box of tampons. Given the incontrovertible presence of menopause, wouldn't it be more practical to buy a package of twenty instead?

A wave of grief arose. The final drops of my menstrual history were before me. Squarely, I faced what might be the last box of tampons in my fertile, female life. God! I did not know how, every day, every moment, for the past fifteen years, John had faced the irreversible loss of his powers.

As sweetly I mourned this passing, albeit still conceptual, women younger than I, and young mothers pushing strollers stuffed with tiny beings, and adolescent girls, all of them braced for future moments of their own, jostled me from reverie. I was in their way. Like John, I was in the way. Suddenly I wearied of the whole business of menstrual management, and wondered if I should buy a two-pound bag of M&M's instead. Where should I park my cart while pondering the box of twenty, the bargain box of one hundred, the two-pound special on Peanut M&M's? It wasn't that much of a leap to worry about where to park myself. I thought of Alice in the Queen Anne Manor, and John in his upright chair, and Helen, presumably in Texas. Where do we park our old, exhausted selves, hungry for rest, for the end of worries, for love? What if the question in the end will be where to park me?

TEN

⇌

The Back Room, or How Not to Die

ANOTHER TRIP TO BETHLEHEMPENNSYLVANIA successfully engineered, I was back home again, where three scant messages awaited me: the first, congratulating me on having won a trip to Las Vegas; the second, from Doug, my alcoholic neighbor, raving about my conducting illicit business from my apartment (that would be my writing), and claiming that any minute he would turn me in; the third, from Harriet, saying she'd found me yet another treasure. She sounded pleased to be honoring her commitment to keep me happily supplied with material. The material in question was Orpha and Herbert Valliet.

My job, as usual, was to ignore what was going on and to cheerfully comply with the preferred version of reality. This made me testy, as I had just failed at this with Mother. The situation that the baffling Valliets presented added helplessness and horror to what clearly was becoming the failure of my quest and nerve.

Herbert sat dying in a darkened room on a brown Naugahyde recliner while his wife, a sturdy Nebraskan, twirled around their little house, pursuing projects toward which to hurl her terror. There was a disconnect between her smile and their dreadful situation. Nor did her pale eyes, the blue of prairie flowers, connect with the lump of sorrow in the back room. I had to wonder, regarding suffering, wasn't there a better way? Was I naive to imagine that suffering might bring two hearts together? It divided the Valliets in two, even as a common shame invited them to step to different rhythms. *That it has come to this,* their shame whispered; that their effort —to be good, to pay their bills in a timely manner, to be churchgoing and believe in God and country—had landed them here, in the awful failure of Herbert's body, seemed to lead, in turn, to bafflement and shame.

Herbert had terrible things wrong with him—diabetes, kidney failure, depression. And every day he went a little blinder. He was becoming a puddle of his own decay. Like being trapped inside your failing systems. Horrible—a horrible way to die. Imagining myself consumed in such a manner, I would pray not to dwell in the awareness. This is how I imagined Herbert spending the time left him—limp and terrified, trapped in the teeth and the claws of his diseases.

As you might imagine, Herbert could do nothing for himself. This gave rise to a curious dialogue between the couple. Orpha, with bright cheer, encouraged him to stay connected to the living world. This drove him into a deepening despair that, coupled with his round-the-clock inertia, launched Orpha's daily bouts of manic cleaning. His reply, in turn, was to clasp a pillow fiercely to his chest and press his silence into further silence. His chair was positioned among flecks of a former self

—old bowling trophies, dusty mugs in the shape of gnomes, a gallon jar of Canadian pennies, a mammoth TV console, and squat transistor radios from the early 1960s. Orpha and I were allowed in for modest and monitored amounts of time in which to dust, during which he issued forth at a crab crawl, scuttling by feel along the countertops, pushing one foot forward with the aid of the other. She tried to cheer him, but nothing bright seized his heart; no effort declared itself worthy of his making.

Orpha exhibited intrepid prairie spunk. In that context, unceasing toil seemed a logical, if ludicrous, outlet. What she really wanted was not *me*, nor the companionship I might offer, so much as a cleaning implement. Now, I like a clean house. I see nothing wrong with routine applications of household products in the maintaining of happy toilet bowls and sparkling sinks and corners radiantly free of dust. Sadly, it is not always possible for me to keep on top of things. Sadly, I am not the one to hire should you want this. Orpha's attraction to domestic projects reminiscent of *I Love Lucy* episodes forced me to draw the line, if not bravely in speech, then passively through strategies of omission. I found more meaning in the message the task suggested. I could not, for example, really get behind scraping the rotting rubber daisies from the bottom of their bathtub. But up they must come—not another day in which these grimy daisies were allowed to attract toe jam, skin flakes, and goo could pass. Such horrors accrued in Orpha's mind to tokens of a world spinning off its axis and undoing in a moment the work of a day. For such rotting rubber daisies a commercial product had been specifically created which of course, she owned, and which upon application boiled up into a grayish-yellow gravy that foamed into toxic slime. No insurance covered me against these hazards. Each visit to Orpha unleashed a novel horror. Once, it was a rug shampooer. This sounds, if not uncomplicated, at least benign. It was not.

"Today," she whispered cheerfully, "I have a puzzle for you." A Hydra-like machine—an intestinal swirl of hosing and suction—was spread all over the kitchen countertops, lips fiercely connected to the faucet.

I looked at Orpha, thinking that I must look deeply, irretrievably forlorn.

"I have never done this before," I whispered hoarsely, but this sabotaged neither her faith in the machine nor her cheer. She continued paging through the instruction booklet, yellowed and brittle, having not seen daylight for 2,700 years. She hooked thingamajigs to thingamabobs, humming. Her excitement was complicated by her hurry to be off to lunch with her church ladies. My time there constituted her weekly break from Herbert.

The Hydra assembled, Orpha grabbed hat and purse and left me. Trying to galvanize, straining to find meaning in the task, I turned on the tap and pressed the button. The machine shuddered like a horse spurred into a geriatric gallop. The howling wind of it did not dent Herbert's slumber. I dragged the hose and its nozzles up the slight rise of dining room floor and to the front of the house. I raked the shaggy carpet. I raked the hoses back and forth over ancient stains.

The tool was disproportionate to the task—a winding, thudding, sucking, elephantine machine set down on a postage-stamp carpet; an overkill cleaning assault on a truly dreadful little house not worth the attention: a one-story bungalow, its floor sinking into damp corners, cramped rooms with stingy windows, a cheap house, a house with no merit whatsoever, a house whose walls before your very eyes were disintegrating, the materials dissolving, the rot insinuating itself in the interstices of poor construction. Oh, this machine was putting me in a vile and bitter mood.

The Hydra exhaled a warm, damp, and dusty stink. It frothed and seemed to sizzle. The dull ocher-colored carpet, its shag suppressed, looked even more defeated than when I'd started. I let the machine puff and strain a little longer. For the sake of Orpha's list, and not wanting Herbert to awake to eerie silence, I let the thing roar on. Finally, I packed it back inside the box and encouraged it to slumber for the next one hundred years.

Last on Orpha's list was to clean the bathroom—in particular, a little patch of floor and wall area behind the toilet. By now, having drawn more than many lines, I refused to do more than a cursory scrape and tidy in this minuscule, dank space just so Orpha would not have to face the ordeal of her husband dying in his recliner. I left fifteen minutes early, spattered with the foul Hydra effluvia and damp tufts of behind-the-toilet dirt.

I would learn later that she inspected my work upon her return. And she made it clear how she felt about my bathroom labor. And she shared this with Harriet. She called her and complained. Her request for a household Hercules had failed to meet her standards. She had discovered *dirt behind the toilet!* and, by way of dramatizing the affront, had fit herself into that tiny wedge of space, scooping my dirt into a baggie. Then she mailed the evidence to Harriet.

Harriet was not happy about the baggie. She explained to Orpha that it had been, indeed, a most unpleasant thing to open. And that, she said, was that.

"You know the truth about this, Hollis?" she asked in her weary, Jewish, *I have seen it all*, New York City voice. "People are insane."

YOU WILL ASK ME, "WHAT IS WRONG WITH ORPHA'S mania in the face of such horror—her husband being eaten alive by his diseases of body and of mind? What is your problem with the machinery of her coping?" If it were her way of claiming a say in the matter—*Ha, Mr. Death, you may occupy the back room, but that doesn't mean that order and cheer must abandon the others*—who would I be to judge? Once again, my romanticized view of the helper role collided with the unflattering reality of my limitations. I will mention, in my defense, Herbert's impenetrability. His gloom had launched my own brand of imagined coping. I vowed hyperbolic rescue. I'd read him the complete works of Shakespeare out loud; I'd convince him to tape-record the highlights of his postal-worker life; I'd present him with a kitten.

It was Orpha's abandonment of thinking that cautioned me. Thinking, which, even in the best of circumstances, so easily unseated by jousting passions, had fled their doom. Orpha was action performed in the service of pushing thought away. No doubt about it, her mindless whirling triggered an awareness of my own. She was my arm-pumping, thigh-thrusting, busy-making, time-killing treks around Bethlehem Steel, the desperate flights out of the Stout household in order to exhaust myself, in order to fall, at night, into bed. To court oblivion, we keep our meters ticking.

I realized that I did not want to think. I did not want to think specifically about *these* matters:

1. Mother. No sooner had I returned home to Seattle than her piteous calls resumed. She had entirely forgotten my latest visit, commanding me, as if I lived one county over, to "come home now!" I lived on borrowed time. It would be only a matter of months before Mother's next crisis.

2. Housing. It would be a matter of *minutes* before living in Belltown became unbearable, before every square inch of open space sported some commercial miasma—not to mention dogs; not to mention parking. When I had returned this time, the old Ivar's clam house on the corner had been replaced by another new condominium, which looked like the new condo one block south, which in turn looked like the less-new but still-quite-new condo one block west of it, and so forth. Yes. I would have to move someday very soon.

3. John. The more involved I was becoming, the more the limitations of my role confronted me. I could share with Harriet anecdotes illustrating my concerns, but in the end, my observations, however persuasive, held no authority with which to help convince his daughters that he had to move. This required an aptitude for witnessing the problematic as it slid toward catastrophe and doing nothing.

BOTH OF OUR BEHAVIORS—ORPHA'S AND MINE—WERE the chronic ruse of progress when one cannot bear to pause and make a better plan. Nor did I want to think about matters even further beyond what I could control. I began this book as a line of selfish inquiry to help my brain gaze, unflinchingly, at what might lie ahead. I was trying to cultivate an acute awareness that I would grow old and someday die, and the bravery to embark on this with skill and muster. How was I doing so far? It wasn't in my cells and viscera, this imminent knowledge of me *aging*. I couldn't relate to John or Orpha as my thirty-years-hence self. They remained *other*. Menopause was proving not to be a bridge. It was proving to be uncomfortable and inconvenient, and if I thought about it, bits of the history of my sexuality—glorious and mortifying both—flickered in mind like previews of a movie, and a door could be heard closing. I meant to find a way to regard aging as something more than closing doors.

It was hard to think about the possibility that my quest was failing. The more I pulled aging into focus—by working with "my" old people, by consenting to return to Bethlehem-pennsylvania again and again, by noting the landmarks of my aging—the more horrible it all appeared. Harrowing. Frightening. Sad.

I might have to rethink my project. I might have to allow for the possibility that this experiment could fail.

ELEVEN

⇌

The Disappointment of
Failed Connections

IN TWO WEEKS, I'D HOST ANOTHER BIRTHDAY AND WAS determined to "turn fifty" once again, to review whether I had learned anything the first time 'round. Inspired by the example of Mary Baker Eddy—who, having declared herself omnipotent, saw no further need for observance of birthdays, simply stopped having them—I decided this year to follow suit. No Christian Scientist worth her salt would ever be trapped by the shrewd falsities of aging. However, my decision didn't discourage Mother from sharing her opinion that to mark my birthday, she would give me a free trip to Guess Where? To enhance the appeal of her invitation, she added, "This will be *your* last birthday that *we* will celebrate together." I reminded her that we'd just completed *her* birthday visit, but she had forgotten. Nor could I protect myself from her gift by saying, in a desperate tone of voice, "I can't take any more time off work!" As we all know, I didn't have work. That is, writing about my mother had become my work, which of course I couldn't tell her, and so I thanked her in advance for the ticket.

But I did manage to require one condition: my parents must engage hospice care in their home. After volumes of insistence that this was nonsense, because Mother did not intend to die, and after many conversations in which it became apparent that they could not bear in mind what hospice really meant, they agreed. Convincing them to accept hospice in their home seemed, at times, my greatest contribution. There were two reasons for this. The first: to admit it's time for hospice is to accept one's prognosis. Their acceptance suggested that the enduring wall of their denial had begun to crumble. And the second: my faith in the spiritual and physical comforts that hospice grants.

THE FIRST THING I DID UPON ARRIVAL WAS TO HATE my father. Having greeted the tiny mother mound lying in a hospital bed downstairs in the living room, I fled into the kitchen to enjoy a hot flash by an open window. I had cranked it open. Hot flash endured, I left the window open for purposes of health and hygiene. Within a minute, it was closed. I inferred the Father's meddling and approached.

"I opened that window a minute ago," I said in a tone suggesting the merest exchange of information. "I need air," I added parenthetically. In the smallest increment of time imaginable, my neutrality devolved to rage and panic.

"There is a cross-draft," he replied. I must point out that no other window in the whole entire house was open. He was a scientist, for God's sake. Surely he knew aerodynamics. "Your mother cannot tolerate a draft."

I must also point out that Mother was sixty feet away in the living room, surrounded by wind-breaking furniture and a large home aide named Margie.

"It is *so* stuffy in here," I cried, rending my garments and sinking to my knees.

The Father, a slight man, a dapper man, who even when relaxing in the home donned professorial attire—ironed shirt and tie—turned to me, as old people will, all of a piece from stem to stern, joints fused, and said, "You may go upstairs. Sit by an open window there." His lips, always moist, pinched in disapproval. The ferocity of his gaze made me think he believed that I was going to kill his wife.

"I came here to spend time with both of you, not to sit in my room upstairs," I said—need I add, lamely?

Ever wary of emotions, the Father tried, when they dared arise, to turn them into stone. He registered our disagreement with a quiver and a widening of the eyes, indicating some force required to control the naughty phenomenon of feelings. "I'm sorry," he said, sounding flat to anyone who might not suspect this. "The draft is too much for Your Mother."

I turned and left the room.

The second thing I did upon arrival was try to rearrange their lives. Mother, as I said, was living in a bed, stationed in the exact middle of the living room. Normally, the living room was a minefield of tchotchkes. Once a pride of formal seating arrangements and Mother's high-end bric-a-brac, the living room had devolved into sickroom clutter—a bedpan the color of dusty rose; plastic washtubs; diapers; the aluminum walker, always in the way; a potty. Logically, the old, decorative detritus should be cleared away to make room for these new and necessary items. And even though the Father spent most of his days recovering from stumbles and near falls due to clutter, no amount of pleading with either parent could convince them that my Terrific Talent for Tidy might be enlisted to tackle the mess.

Adding to the clutter was the home aide, Margie. A big woman of limited mental acumen, she was the sort of person whose raison d'être, without any gift for follow-through, was to be *needed*—a perfect match for Mother. Margie seemed always to be sucking on a pebble, and between her mysterious sucking, smacking noises, platitudes would dribble out, carried on a voice wavery and hollow. I would hear her coach Mother to forget what the hospice nurse had said, by way of preparing her for death. "You have to put it out of your mind, Elizabeth," she said, rumbling with indignation while administering a therapeutic pummel to Mother's tissue-paper triceps. Her tightly permed, fuzzy, bowl-shaped hair quivered with the effort. I went up to my bedroom and did a hundred push-ups. It was precisely Mother's limited time, Mother's actual decline, that I wanted hospice to insert as the reality, and that had, prior to the Margie obstruction, afforded a respite from my parents' denial. What did I owe them, anyway? If Mother wanted Margie over Truth, so what? I started in on sit-ups.

The third thing I did was hope, vigorously, for the Important Chat.

"How do you think I'm feeling?" Mother asked Margie after the pummeling. She closed her eyes, ready to receive the lemon drop of reassurance. "Are my feet too hot?" She twitched them, as Margie bent to scrutinize a sock. Finally Margie left, dragging off the suffocating weight of her concern. Mother, rosy with her beating, turned toward me and crooked a finger. *Here it is*, I thought as I drew near. *The Chat*.

"Tell me how I look, " she said, gazing up at me. Now, I have studied Mother's demise for years, witnessing the gap between how she looks, actually, and how she wants to be seen, and so I was not seduced into believing that she was asking me how she looked, *actually*. And I have witnessed Mother asking many folks this question—the pastor, the nurses and the doctors, the Father, friends, and me—but it wasn't honesty she sought. Mother, tethered to oxygen, able to arise from bed only to be swiveled out and onto the potty, with bedhead to beat the band, now weighing seventy-measly-six pounds, for God's sake, *did not look good*!

I thought I'd fiddle with the truth. "How do you mean?" I asked, thinking that if she had to repeat the question, she'd hear what she was asking.

"How do I look?" she asked again. "Tell me how I look."

Her thinning hair was two-toned—two inches of natural white that pushed away, from the roots, her old, dyed-chestnut color, and the hair of the back of her head stood straight up like a baby's. Flakes of skin around her brow, forehead, and scalp made me want to take a dining table crumber and gently brush them off. Her eyes floated in a moist green haze.

I said, "You look exhausted."

Her body jerked; her eyes flashed little sparks. "What?" she said. In the Whitman's Sampler of my mother's question, I'd offered a chocolate-covered jelly to the preferred coconut cream.

"Exhausted," I repeated, enunciating clearly.

"Exhausting?" Her eyes grew sly.

I tried another angle. "Fatigued," I said.

"*You're* fatigued?" she asked warily.

"No, you," I said. "*You're* fatigued."

"It's true, I can't run anymore," she said.

"You never liked to run," I said drily.

A puzzled, frightened look crept into her eyes. She began to ramble about the nurse, who had told her she was dying. "Everybody's giving up on me," she said. "Everybody thinks I'm useless." I had spoken with the nurse, Pat, a woman grounded in kindness and gentle humor, and I knew that the mission of hospice is to help patients bring acceptance to their process as best they can and in their own individual manners. Between the fatuity and the Christian Science, Mother offered considerable challenges, but I had no doubt that Pat's only agenda was to help give Mother as good and as cogent an experience of her dying as could be imagined.

"Who's saying you're useless?" I asked.

"What?" she said, blinking, as if I had started the conversation. "Tell me, do you think it's hopeless?" she asked desperately. "I know I have to have hope, and if I don't . . ." She trailed off.

I came to Bethlehempennsylvania neither to offer false reassurance nor to be unkind. I let long Pauses of Uncertainty cling and cluster. What did I know about death? "I don't think of hope and hopelessness when it comes to living and dying," I said, noting how it made me flinch to say "dying" out loud, to admit into the room a trumpet, a trombone, that had not yet been sounded. Dying—as if this soft-sounding word, the sound of rotting fruit, could somehow hurt her feelings.

"I don't think of hope and hopelessness in relation to living or dying," I said again. "I just think of it as going to another place." Did I? No matter how hard I tried, it was impossible to think of death with the same kind of certainty, the same arrangement of feeling and anticipation, as, say, dinner. My mind was convinced that I wasn't going to die. Nor, in Mother's mind, was she.

She drew herself up, trembling. "Watermelon," she said with such a burst of feeling that it almost knocked her on her side. "I want watermelon."

"It's too early, Mom," I said. "It's only April."

"I want to live," she said.

"Nobody wants to die," I said. "It's the hardest thing in the world to do."

She nodded, as if letting this tiny bite of understanding slip underneath her tongue. She looked into my face sharply. "What's wrong with your eye?" she asked.

It's true, I was crying—albeit discreetly. Maybe half a dozen tears in this handholding, deeply gazing little talk.

"I'm crying, Mum. It's what happens when people are moved."

Blink. "What?"

"I'm *moved*," I all but shouted.

"Oh," she whispered, nodding, and blinked again, gathering her thoughts. "What do you think of us?" she asked.

That stopped my mind. "Us." Our Perfect Family? Our secret-driven history? "We have become," I lied, "very close."

And then Mother prayed. My lie inspired a little riff on the Lord's Prayer. "Oh, Father," she gushed, "thank You for having brought us all together, and guided us, and made the right decisions for us," and so forth, and I was thinking, Gee, *You could have done a little better by my education than Lake Erie College*, but I would not linger in this train of thought, because what about the Whole Adoption Thing? I mean that had been no picnic.

Radiant with prayer, she opened her eyes. "Watermelon," she said again, and again I said, "It's April. You'll have to wait." But Mother had no tolerance for waiting.

"I no longer wish to speak with this person," she said, and closed her eyes.

TWELVE

⇌

Riddles Abound in Resolution

I HARBORED NO DELUSION OF A MORE CANDID AND emotionally satisfying rapport with the Other Mother, the one from whom I was expelled. I knew this. Plagued by the consequences of knowing nothing about my birth and all attendant details, I had finally tracked her down. *You* have probably walked around all your life in the skin of physical belonging; I have walked around in wonder. So, initiating a search for my mother, Phyllis, was like mounting a presidential campaign, organizing the assault on the Matterhorn, or preparing for a whole year of advanced study in the later works of Henry James. Finding her was not what I expected.

The Other Mother lived in Salem, Oregon, and, as far as I know, still does. If she's still alive, I do not know it. I have a brother, Brian, whom she would not let me meet. I've seen some photographs. He looks like me, but younger.

When Phyllis and I agreed to meet each other, I'm sure neither of us knew what to expect. Maybe she wanted assurance that giving up her baby had been the good, the right thing to do. Maybe I wanted to get a long and legitimate look at her, compare our hair, breasts, and noses, and then wring her neck. I don't know. I know only that I had to do it.

I had located her, written her a letter, which she failed to answer, and, deterred but still determined, journeyed west to stand before my flesh and blood. I made the first phone call from a terrible town called Eureka. Not surprisingly, it was in California. Hot for the auspicious, I believed that this name, and a pack of Lucky Strikes, would bring me courage and good fortune. It worked. We talked a long time. She'd been waiting for my call after getting the letter, she said. She apologized for being a lousy correspondent. She said she'd like to meet me someday. I said, "How about tomorrow?" She paused to pick herself up off the floor and we agreed to meet for lunch.

And so we met. It was 1979, the hottest day that summer in Salem, Oregon. I was early, having lost all sense of time. Dazed, I waited. All the waiting of my life had led to this. The pavement was the waiting. Salem, Oregon, was every corner in every town or city I had ever waited in. Phyllis was everyone I had waited for. Outside the restaurant, I waited, kneeling to fuss with the buckle of my sandal.

A shadow fell over me. "I thought you were a boy," the voice belonging to the shadow said, and I looked up and saw a woman with short gray hair. "I thought you were a boy," the voice repeated. A set of warm brown eyes looked over an enormous pair of breasts. The eyes were a lighter brown than mine, and in that moment, *my moment*, I felt no rush of recognition that I had always hungered for, even while ascertaining that this woman was my mother.

"I'll buy you lunch. It's the least I can do," the woman

with the breasts and the light brown eyes, my mother, said.

In the restaurant, a preponderance of maroon reigned—the rug, the curtains, the round lamp hanging above the table, casting a thin cone of light over the ersatz grain of our Formica table. I was trying to force the emergence of myself from my mother's features. It was a hell of a first thing to say—*I'll buy you lunch. It's the least I can do.* Here I was again, with another mother, about to instigate another failed connection over lunch. Furtively we cast looks toward each other.

"Actually, I would have recognized you anywhere," Phyllis said. "What are you going to order?"

I dropped my gaze to the oversize, laminated menu and hid behind the luncheon entries. "The tuna melt," I said.

When the food came, I was more interested in poking it than eating.

"Tell me about yourself," Phyllis said briskly.

I watched her chew. Unlike the Stouts, Phyllis seemed not to slip through the world on a priority of good manners. She ate noisily.

"What do you want to know?" I asked, picking up my sandwich. Its warmth was spongy and abhorrent, and I put it down. "I was not raised Italian. My parents are the Stouts—Betty and Robert. They're nice." I kept my words and inflection on a leash, afraid of sounding whiny. "They've given me a lot," I said in sum, as if pointing out the advantages of nurture over nature. "Tell me about you."

I had thought I would have a million questions at the ready: *What time was I born? Who were my grandparents? Who is my family?* I had thought they would come tumbling out—a ragged line, jockeying for position. But no. I could hardly keep my eyes open, and when I did, I could not shake the blur.

She started talking about her father in Connecticut, and I fought a wave of drowsiness. His name was Eugene, I heard her say. Amazingly, I didn't care. All my life I had imagined such a moment, when, as with an open-mouthed and starving baby bird, information and nourishment would be poured in. All I wanted now was to disappear, to sleep. His name was Eugene. It had no meaning.

"I loved him," Phyllis said. "He taught me to speak Italian. To be a Guinea-WOP then in Connecticut, you realize . . ." She trailed off. Her chin dipped abruptly to emphasize the point. "He had a garden, bless the man. He managed to grow eggplant and tomatoes in Connecticut."

Suddenly I snapped out of it. Suddenly I loved Eugene. I sat in the gladness of this new knowledge and the grief of never having known or been known by this man. I tore into my tuna melt.

The bill came, and we both reached for it. In the scramble, it fluttered to the floor. I retrieved it; "$8.75," it said. *My mother has treated me to an $8 lunch*, I thought sadly. *Closer to $10, if you count the tip.* The Stouts would never be caught dead in a place like this. Not even in an emergency. I knew it.

WE DECIDED TO EXTEND OUR AGONY BY GOING FOR A walk. There was a park. It offered shade, the space through which to ramble and further dip into this strange phenomenon —perfect strangers, joined in the most fundamental way, whom chance had caused to part. I couldn't reconcile the two, chance and the woman beside me. "Mother" was too big a term for what she was.

I kept wanting to drink her in, noting the details: curly

hair, worn short; enormous earlobes hanging like a Buddha's; the large, hooked nose. A path led through a wooded section of cedar, towering hemlock, and Douglas fir and rose up toward a rhododendron grove. The blooms, profuse, floated like airborne, crumpled tissues. Intuiting that Phyllis's capacity to entertain my curiosity was on a short fuse, I asked, "What was it like in Philadelphia, what you went through, back then, in the . . . *home* and all?"

She hurled a sound outward and scaled it back to a shrill laugh. "Oh, my, it was a circus—all those crazy girls from all over, waiting it out. Just awful. There's not that much to tell."

"Oh," I said, ridding my voice of expectation.

"You were expecting maybe happy memories?" Phyllis snapped.

We passed a woman in an apricot-colored wig. She was extracting crumbs from a crumpled bag and flinging them at pigeons.

"We made the best of a bad thing back there," she continued. "All of us girls were just waiting to get out, or die, I guess, although no one actually said it." She had changed her tone to one less brittle.

I reached for my mother's words as if they were butterflies. I shivered. It was almost too cool in the woods. I wondered if Phyllis had heard herself call me a "mistake," a "bad thing." Before this, my *moment*, I had believed I wanted truth. I couldn't have known its impact. I think I still believed it was better to know the worst than to live in ignorance.

"I've decided to take my name," I said. "The name you gave me."

"No kidding! What for?" Phyllis asked after a wary pause.

"I love it," I said. "Because I love my name."

My mother looked at me quickly, and then away.

"My name is the most treasured thing I own," I said, trying for lightness.

The air carried the scent of warm pine, sweetened by lilies and roses. "What time was I born?" I persevered.

"What?" Phyllis asked, and gave a laugh that almost split my eardrums. "I don't remember *that*." She snapped the "that" like the end of a wet towel.

Everything I valued seemed to have slipped my mother's mind. "I don't understand," I said softly. "I thought that was something a woman does not forget."

"We were put in white rooms, white walls, white floors, no clocks, nothing. Too much was happening. Who could keep track?" she said.

Enough, I thought. It was exhausting, all I could not say. I stopped, unable to maintain the delicate steps, skirting such issues as might upset her. It was impossible to be just pissed off, pure and simple. Something beautiful was dying—a hummingbird, a sunny day. Suddenly I knew it was my fantasies that were dying. No more fantasizing "Mother." Beside me stood fact, with her bad hair and enormous earlobes.

Revulsion silenced me. I hated how my mother looked— not like a gorgeous Italian movie star, not like Sophia Loren. I shuddered to think that Phyllis's breast fate could so easily have been mine. She was not my dream mother. She did not radiate the August heat of female sensuality. I had thought that information would have bathed me in relief, that blithely I'd zip off the top of my head and let my mother shower me with stories, the "us" of things. But my appetite had limits. It even had a shape. It was a tiny mole that could progress only quarter inches at a time through darkness.

Of course, I had my Crucial Question: *Why the fuck did you give me up?* I skirted it, because of terror. I was terrified of falling through the ice, into the black, raging water of our shared misery. What would we do there? Who would rescue whom? Who could linger in such feelings? Their foundation was birth—less than an inch in a whole life span, and so primal, how can you go back? Should I tear off my clothes, flop on my back, wiggle my limbs, and cry? The feelings were way back there. They did not have college degrees or wear mascara.

We paddled back to the land of safer matters (food preferences, literature, awful jobs) and continued to walk around the park until it was all one blur of predictability—the order of ball field, hill, amalgam drinking fountain on the right, woods, and then out again into the more tended grounds of picnic tables and fire grills, around the periphery, past the rhododendrons and the apricot wig bobbing over crumbs, out to the roses, back down into the gloomy woods. The past mingled with the present. My craving for a past mingled with Phyllis's protection of it. Secrets. We walked in the crossfire of secrets, and yet there was no crescendo of relief.

I knocked cautiously on memory's door; I never asked directly, *So, what did I smell like? What was it like in "the home"? Tell me about the other women. How did you pass the time waiting to give birth to me? Why the fuck did you leave?*

"Are you married?" Phyllis asked.

"No," I said.

"You're lucky," she said, laughing harshly. "We fight all the time, Lou and me. Of course, this hasn't been easy for Brian. He hates it when we yell."

"Brian," I said back. "Brian?"

"He'll be seventeen this March. Same as me. An Aries."

"An Aries," I said. "Same as me."

"Oh, yeah," said Phyllis.

"You didn't forget *my* birthday?" I asked jokingly, afraid that, yes, she had. I did not shout, "I have a brother!" That would have established an entitlement to call my kin *kin*. I did not dare ask, "May I meet him?" Besides, I hated the name Brian—simply hated it.

"Two hours every morning in the bathroom, blow-drying his hair," she droned, still describing his pathologies. "I bang on the door. He tells me to get lost. He locks it. Sometimes it gets so bad I have to go tell Lou to drag him out. It's disgusting."

She sounded genuinely miserable, and it made me wonder if she was giving these examples of unhappiness so that I wouldn't feel so pathetically rejected. Maybe this was her way of being kind.

"Do you think I could see a picture?" I asked, trying to sound as if this were innocuous, like asking for a chip.

"Sure," said Phyllis, with a vague flutter of her hand.

Each question I asked skirted the edges of this one: *Why the fuck did you give me up?* This question was buried so deeply in my organs, it had gotten metabolized as doubt, anxiety, workaday paranoia. It had become the way I viewed myself and my relations, the world around me and what of it I could and could not have.

Why the fuck did you give me up?

And then it was time for us to part again. Drained of every little drop of curiosity and caring, I just wanted Scotch, lots and lots of Scotch. And to return to the half-smoked package of Lucky Strikes. And to hole up somewhere for an endless evening. And to think. To try to think.

"Listen, I'm really glad you did this," she was saying. "I'm really glad we had this visit."

What the fuck do you want from me? Now, there might have been her companion question.

If you can't tell me why you left, at least give me my goddamn stories. That seemed reasonable enough. As you can see, I was very, very pissed off.

It was an impossible question, razor sharp. The sort that exerted a contradictory pull toward both protective ignorance and a concrete answer. It was an "Are you having an affair?" type of question. You don't want to bring it up, but you can't put it out of your mind. There it hangs, charging the air between the most innocuous request or question: "Where are you going?" "Where have you been?" You want and do not want to know.

Why the fuck did you give me up?

Because I couldn't handle having a baby. Well, okay, but if this might be the answer, it would serve as well to keep the whole thing abstract. It gave nothing of the torment of her decision—loving how I smelled; smitten by the same brown eyes she had; in awe of what she saw of my father in my smile or tiny worry line. It offered nothing to relate to as a little being.

In the end, upon parting as two grown women, we experienced not catharsis so much as relief. I had not killed my mother. She hadn't fallen apart in the encounter, collapsing underneath the old grief and the guilt and the torment of keeping secrets. Perhaps the best that can be said of our reunion is we survived it.

⇌

Commentary:

LOST, TUMBLED, SEEKING, SOUGHT

LOOKING BACK, THIRTY-FIVE YEARS LATER, I DON'T
know if that was entirely so. I couldn't *not* have done it, having
obsessed about finding my mother from the moment I was
told, "You are adopted." When stated, the word oozed a weird,
not-normal tone. To which, quickly, would be appended, "We
love you, you are our special *special* little girl."

Four years old, five, I seem to remember, and then the race
was on. Then, in 1979, I found her, did the thing I had
imagined would hand me the dazzling mosaic of a self, and
instead the bits that were handed had a more shattering than
integrating effect.

What had I hoped to gain? The satisfaction of a driving
curiosity. The solid ground of recognition. A self that cohered
through physical resemblances and history; to make connection with the pre-Stout self, a self issued from the wet tussle
and tangle of sex.

There is no getting away from it, from sex, and for as long
as I remember, I wondered if my parents even had it. Somehow
I was related to this; somehow I sensed a lack of sex between
them. I knew from a very early age that my parents had not
gotten me in the "normal" way. Other parents exuded a kind of
mammalian warmth that mine lacked. There was, for me, a
different feeling between my best friend, Susan Conard's,
parents and mine. Susan and her two younger sisters looked

like the perfect mix and match, begotten from George and Caroline. Each girl had clusters of distinct George-Caroline characteristics. There was no mistaking that sex had made the girls. My parents exuded formality and form; their bond seemed contractual. They were devoted to each other, but their touch lacked fire. I had a deep and wary knowledge that I was not *of* them, had not issued forth from sex, did not contain their material. I had arrived a bundle all my own, albeit from an unknown source.

I became fixated on their neat twin beds; I never saw them share a bed. I never saw them touch with anything more than sweet regard. I got angry at what I believed to be the lack of sex between them, as if it were their failure at it that had produced my unhappiness.

So, one thing I hoped to gain in meeting Phyllis was a sense of being embodied. I wanted to embody myself, to stop feeling adrift both in my body and in the Stout penumbra. What else did I hope to gain? An experience of recognition— the shock of recognizing her/my face, her/my body, whether the similarities would occur in ankles/hands/eyes. I wanted the shock of recognizing my source. I wanted to *be* recognized, as if mere physical resemblance might confer the deepest satisfaction of being seen and known. I wanted the recognition of my beginning; the impossible re-creation of that first moment of arrival into the world: *Hello. Welcome.* I wanted the early emptiness erased.

SO, IN THE SUMMER OF 1979, IN SALEM, OREGON, IN record-breaking heat, we finally came together. I had yearned for this all of my conscious and unconscious life. I was finally here—*here* with its blistering details, bizarrely over lunch. Yearning had caught up with fact. Yearning had defined me, had begun, almost, to constitute a talent. Yearning and its fulfillment collided; I was a rider thrown through the air, hitting the ground hard, my brain in its hard pan reverberating with the sudden stop.

I grew sleepy, dim-witted, imagined lowering my head onto the table. Exhaustion overtook my curiosity. I swung between intensity and torpor, the dissonance of engaging after thirty years of not. The shock that my search had ended contributed to this back-and-forth between intensity and torpor. It was like taking a vacation from consciousness, retreating into thick lethargy as my mind processed information bit by bit, trying to comprehend and categorize terms like "brother," "*your* grandfather Eugene," "my mother was a cold Yankee bitch." I'd get capsized, then, by swells of feeling.

There must be a term for this, when the effort to connect and the self-protective resistance to connection create a riptide moment. I wonder what she felt. Perhaps our riptides doubly, triply crashed over and underneath each other's. I brought no skill to this; I was completely unprepared, in spite of years of preparation—reading, joining activist adoptee movements and subsequent groups, attending conferences. None of this came to my rescue. Nor was it possible to relinquish a kind of false camaraderie, to jettison the feigned merriment and nonchalance, the adherence to social norms, the pretense of appetite and normalcy—two grown women bearing a resemblance to each other, mother and daughter with absolutely nothing but biology as bridge.

I did not know, in these moments, how I felt. I was too full of feeling. It would take two years to regroup and recover, to let pieces fall into place, into a brand-new place called biological assurance. That is how it felt. I had my little bio-patch to stand on, and it felt like something I could tend proudly. I could begin to grow something of my very own on it.

What were our parting words, really? There was a visceral dissonance between the feigned casualness of language and of posture, as if this meeting were nothing more than coffee and a walk with a friend. Did the blood-and-bone parts of our mother-daughter bond find any comfort? Warily, we examined each other. In truth, she was a stranger. I tallied our resemblances eagerly, though—features, gestures, bursts of manic laughter. We maintained a sheen of civility and cool. Was this a cool thing to do, or crazy? Who knew? I thought I should feel one way and suppressed feeling another. The words that we could not say to each other were indeed more pronounced. The raw "whys?" The tormented "becauses."

I wanted to fall in love with the Other Mother, to return to some imagined place of safety and wholeness. But she was as broken and nervous as I.

In distilling the essence of disappointment, I have not, thus far, included the moments with Phyllis of recognition and joy. What we had in common—our lopsided, zigzag, slapstick stabs at gainful employment; humor, flashily expressed; lean, spare calves affixed to knobby knees; a tendency to pile books on all available surfaces; an energy not Stout-recessed but that leaned forward, almost pouring from the eyes—made me want to magnify, exaggerate, the commonality. We shared a hyper-bolic disdain for zonal geraniums and daisies; a worship of garlic, that bulb so deeply distrusted by the Stouts, eschewed in Pennsylvania Dutch cooking, and thought to be possibly satanic. Entering, for the first time, her tiny ocher house on

Waldo Avenue, a large, scowling crack across the lintel, I noticed a book plethora. Topping a slithering pile was Eudora Welty's latest, which I, too, was in the process of reading. There was a thrill as these correspondences spontaneously turned up. *Watch it*, my heart said, or should have said, *easy to force the connection from such slender threads of gladness.* I didn't know the extent of my wish that the connection might deepen.

In looking back, I see that focusing on one aspect of our reunion (that would be rejection) allowed me to overlook the pleasantries and the relief our similarities afforded. Those shards and tidbits seduced me, encouraging a belief that we'd be doing this forever, that over time we'd come closer to each other and cultivate, or salvage, a relationship from this primal bond.

I REALIZE I HAVE BEEN WAITING FOR MY APOLOGY. EVEN now, when in a typically anxious frame of mind, I find that my thoughts shop among rows of minor grievances, alighting on a memory of a slight, perhaps—something of no great significance but nonetheless fodder for my perseveration.

My mind will pick it out like a blouse, fingering the fabric, patting the wound. Majestically, I wait for an email offering the gift of contrition. It's all so arbitrary, my mind's hunt for redress. The point is I keep waiting for apologies, *the* apology—the call from my brother, whom Phyllis might have told, "You have a sister. We have met. Perhaps you'd like to meet her." I wait for her to say, "I'm sorry I kept you a secret from your brother, my husband, and myself." For how can you abandon your two-month-old baby, believing you have kept her a secret from the world, and not wall off a continent of yourself in order to *get on with it*, however faltering your steps?

I wait for the apology from the Stouts, even from their graves. I imagine this in the form of wealth long hidden, suddenly found; of documents unearthed, revealing their hopes, their stories. I keep expecting the phone to ring and to hear Phyllis saying, "I'm sorry. I said terrible things. I've actually thought about you every single day," as if the past tense would mean she had jettisoned denial and launched us into the present.

But what, after all, would "sorry" bring?

I believe in the release forgiveness bequeaths in a final moment. I believe that it doesn't take much.

We carefully did not speak of the most urgent things between us—the bond that must have existed in the pregnancy, in the birth, in the first gaze and the subsequent holdings. We did not speak of that which surely, however brief, meant love, nor did we speak of her ambivalence. Was it instant? Or had it simmered so long, gestating along with me, that birth only intensified it? My birth would have made a choice imperative, and how would she have made it? Whom would she have told; who would have helped? I remember the palpability of her relief when I said, "The Stouts have been very good to me. It all turned out okay"—a placid shorthand meant to reassure her.

"Oh"—she gave a long sigh—"I'm so glad to hear that. I worried and worried. I always wondered if I made the right choice."

I cannot imagine. I am not a mother; I decided against this firmly, *firmly*, when I was thirteen. Gym class was ending, and the girls, donning their bras and slips, tossed out avid, avaricious comments about the boys. I was alert, listening.

Karen Blickwede stated that she couldn't wait to breed and have six or seven children at the least. I thought, *No. Ugh. Gross. No way, not me.* I saw in a flash where it and I could so easily be headed—boyfriends and kissing and college and sex and marriage and family, and *no.* This trajectory held no joy. So, no, I cannot viscerally imagine what it must be like to give up your child. I only know it as the give-up-ee. In Phyllis's palpable relief, I glimpsed the scale of the event in her life and how it must always have dogged her.

WORDS, LAST WORDS—HOPE AND DREAD CLOTHED IN platitudes:

"We'll do this again." *(Yes, but not too soon.)*

"I am so glad we . . ." *(What? Met? Got together? Had lunch after all these years?)*

Since I had not yet moved from Philadelphia to Seattle—indeed, had not yet made the decision at all and was only on my way up there to spend a few weeks with a college friend—I could not say, "Your turn. Come up and see me in Seattle." But when I did make the move a few months later and had again gone to Salem to see her, I did say, "Your turn to come up and visit me."

She replied, "No, I don't think so. I can't get away from Lou, and besides, he needs the car. And I haven't told him. We'll have to wait till he dies, I'm afraid"—harsh laugh—"but really, when I'm free, we'll spend more time together."

After our initial reunion, I, reeling, stepped up into the plane and ordered a double Scotch as soon as it was possible. Phyllis? What feelings enveloped her as she drove home to the house on Waldo Avenue, her secret more or less materialized?

And yet this secret had still to be maintained. She would always keep the news of me from Lou and Brian. Did my tracking her down bring her any joy? signal the possibility of freedom from the weight of the old secret? Or was it the sound of the other shoe finally dropping?

YEARS WOULD GO BY. AFTER I MADE HALF A DOZEN VISITS to Salem, listlessness and a vague annoyance followed. My relationship with Phyllis would not progress. She refused to reveal more of herself to me; she continued to keep me a secret from Lou and Brian. She could never drive up to Seattle, because "what would I tell Lou?" She required I not put my name on the envelopes of the letters I wrote her, nor send photographs. And then when Lou died and she still made no offer to visit me, I realized that I had been waiting, and was always waiting, to be claimed.

In 1993, I wrote her my last letter. I had not intended it as such. I asked to know more about my grandfather Eugene. What little I knew suggested affinities. Could she thus tell me more?

Scene: Seattle, 1993

A LONG, BUILT-IN DESK LOOKING OUT OF WALL-LENGTH WINDOWS at the mountains across the sound—snowcapped but not entirely covered, it being August.

I am writing to Phyllis, diplomatically framing two requests. I never know how she'll respond to my questions. I want two things: information about my grandfather Eugene and to meet my brother. I believe I must express these desires in prose that charms and justifies. My words must be ambassadors.

I am entitled to these things, I think. Surely she must feel a shred of maternal obligation. What, in truth, do I feel for her?

Nothing, I believe, but what she owes me. I feel terrifically owed, and in that grip, there is no room for her.

Occasionally I privilege the mountain view over my writing. I am here because of her, I think. Seattle is a lot closer to Salem, Oregon, than Philadelphia is.

I write my long letter, encase the two requests in earnest prose, trying to explain this great blood yearning to belong. I sign it, seal it, and wait. Nothing about this big, elegant house I am caring for with my partner Alex, while friends, the owners, are on sabbatical in England is permanent. We are squatting in two places—this large elegance and a shabby little cabin on Lopez Island.

Scene: Lopez, Driving to a Meeting

I HOLD PHYLLIS'S LETTER; HER RESPONSE HAS COME. I have held it for a while, reluctant to open it. It feels angry and thick. I ask Alex to read it, but she is driving.

"Pull over," I say. "You read it. I'll drive."

She pulls onto the shoulder, dislodging fragrance from the grasses. The quinces are blooming; the sky is azure. She begins:

"'This letter will be brief; it will also state things you should know but probably won't be able to accept. I am getting tired of your relentless pursuit!'"

There is a pause that lengthens. "What?" I say. "Go on."

"I can't," she says. "I can't read any more of it out loud."

"Is it awful?"

"It is not kind."

I pull over. We change places. I read. The letter is not long; its contents feel long. The ink is blue; the force behind the blue words is such that the pages bear deep impressions. Various phrases are underlined, such as:

" . . . relentless pursuit . . ."

" . . . .no place in each other's lives . . ."

" . . . just let go . . ."

Among others. She might as well have underlined the whole damn thing.

Unlike mine, her handwriting is terrific—cursive, legible, round, yet firm. I take in the force, the underlining, but not the content.

Fisherman's Bay flashes by, one of those astonishing August afternoons—the sky a blindingly bright, clean blue. Light shards fall on the water in diamond shapes. Everything sparkles—the needles of the pines, the bending yellow grasses, the wingtips of the gulls. Fragrances speed by. Occasionally they linger, allowing identification—fennel, seaweed, brine. Once again, I've been rejected. I don't frame it thus; there is no frame in this moment. It is a trick, I tell myself, of a large and baffling nature.

Gravel crunching underneath the weight of other cars and my dragging feet, we walk across the parking lot. How can I sit in a meeting with a normal face, looking out with normal eyes? How can language issue from this? In the room, where there is a heartbreaking lack of sunlight, words and chatter drift from far away. I excuse myself, apologizing. I say a tiny bit about why. I excuse myself from those seated close to me at the table. I excuse myself and say that I will now leave to go drink vodka.

The small clutch of those from whom I have excused myself are now at another table—at the Islander, ordering vodka and presumably, wisely, some food to go with it. I do not remember.

I have been romancing blood for over sixty years. Blood-longing; longing to blood-belong. Longing to belong to a tribe whose members you could point at and say, admiringly, "Oh, those McGillicuddy eyes; that nose passed down from the patriarch; those raven tresses."

I was sensitive to friendly lies. By the time I was four, it seemed, the ruse had been established. I was said to have my father's eyes, my mother's chin. And at four, I did not buy it, and why not? Why did it matter? Why the big blood deal? It never ceased to matter; it became the nattering narrative, the supreme grievance. I needed to find my blood—blood, tribe, family. I could have been a fish, a creature with one scaly arm and the other made of feathers; a half-thing; a mockery.

It remains the strangest thing, to share a bit of blood with perfect strangers.

An image: as I gazed at a photo of my brother Brian in young adolescence, I saw, or believed I saw, a resemblance in hands, in jaw, and felt an instant gratification that grew quickly into an urge to meet him. What really was that urge? A rush of integrating recognition; a feeling of being tethered to the planet.

Having wooed, courted, found, having devoted years to the grail of it, I see—from my Stout view—a paradox. Yearning has to coexist with gratitude. I am materially and educationally better off, have been given opportunities that would not have been possible with my "source parents."

For example, Amsterdam.

I was a little girl, and we were in Europe for the first time. It was 1954, and I was six. We were sitting in a wonderfully enormous, plush hotel in Amsterdam. The air of the hotel would be, for me, the signature fragrance of Europe, at least of Europe's indoor, public spaces—freshly baked, crusty bread mingling with the dust of thick carpets and upholstery. The carpet was plush, the lighting stately and, even then, old fashioned. I was allowed dessert, for I had cultivated a passion for this dessert at this particular Amsterdam hotel: ice cream, superior to what we'd get at home—rich, dense, creamy—over which the waiter, in a tux, poured thick, hot chocolate sauce from a small silver pitcher. He performed this from a great height, rhythmically lifting and letting drop his arm, so that the chocolate fell in a slender, braided stream. Over the heavenly concoction, he arranged a nest of spun brown sugar.

As the sacrament unfolded, I noticed, at a table for two, on my left at ten o'clock (I'd just learned how to tell time), an elegant silver man and a woman with high hair and festooned with jewelry.

"It's Hoppy," I said.

My parents stared at ten o'clock. "No. That can't be Hoppy."

"Yes, it is, too," I said. I knew my cowboys and heroes.

In and around each other and dessert, we peered. Was it? It certainly looked to be Hopalong Cassidy, my idol of the moment.

"Maybe we could ask Hoppy for his autograph, shall we?" And then my father made magic, rising with ease from his chair to address the Hopalong table. A greeting; words exchanged. I had momentarily abandoned the sundae. He was approaching with an outstretched arm and a smile. It *was*

Hoppy, so silver and handsome, and he shook my hand, and I was dizzy with the prominence of that moment. He slipped his hand underneath his white jacket and pulled out a Hopalong Cassidy coin. He bowed and took his wife's elbow, and they departed.

Soon we would follow, as evenings ended early; I was a little girl, and my parents were attentive. I would beg to ride the elevator up and down for as long as they could tolerate my begging. They were patient but had their parental needs. We stepped into the magic chamber, all polished brass and glass; the guts of it, the gears and cables, revealed that mix of elegance and its underpinnings. I got to push buttons and slide open and shut the clattering metal gate. I got to squeal as the chamber lurched into action—the ride down terrifying, the ride up labored.

Now, had I been the child of Phyllis, raised in Bristol, Connecticut, or Berkeley, California, or Salem, Oregon, none of this would have happened. Issues of blood and lineage aside, I'm bothered by these questions of class and opportunity.

Edgar: A Story

ALL TO BE LEARNED ABOUT MY FATHER WAS DELIVERED in bursts and stages—the first, my birth certificate, procured in 1979 in Philadelphia (EDGAR OSBORNE; AGE: 31; BIRTH-PLACE: CANADA); then from Phyllis ("he had red hair and he drank too much") in Salem, Oregon; and finally from his widow, Florine, in Beaver City, Nebraska, fifteen years later. She would be by far the most forthcoming and generous of sources.

All three players came of age in Bristol, Connecticut. Florine and Edgar were engaged. She joined the WAAC and flew over the Atlantic, blacking out and vomiting into her helmet with all the rest ("Gee, I wish they would have warned us about that"); saw Paris; returned and resumed the engagement. She and her sister were asked, then, to leave for California to help their aging father. She called off the engagement; it seemed unfair to dangle in the uncertainty of her return; plus, "I got cold feet." In the interim, between her departure and unexpected return, occurred Phyllis.

I knew even less about that narrative than I did about Florine, who had been, up to the spring of 1994, a perfect and unnamed stranger.

Phyllis and Edgar connected. I commenced. Florine returned. Phyllis left for Philadelphia, making off with her secret.

When my mother found herself pregnant in the early fall of 1947, she would have faced ostracism and scandal, or so she must have believed, as this news would not be shared, happily or not, with a husband. She left home to endure her pregnancy in Germantown, Pennsylvania, in the Florence Crittenden Home for Unwed Mothers. This was a social do-good-uplift institution, founded in 1896, to help unwed mothers (a.k.a. "lost and fallen women and wayward girls") who, victims of the times, would have been typically sent away to endure their shameful pregnancies and have their babies. By the 1930s, with sixty-two homes, the establishment evolved policies to forge relationships with official adoption agencies. Adoption was touted as the better choice.

⇌

HAVING FOUND PHYLLIS, WHICH, IN TURN, REQUIRED recovering from finding Phyllis, I put any interest in further exploration on major pause. I had sustained a plaintive and lingering wish to meet my brother but was advised to search for my father first, as time seemed more the essence.

His is an odd name—Edgar Nehemiah Osborne. I bore no curiosity about him initially. Then I did. In the pause, energy collected itself, taking the time it needed for the next surge. But I found him too late. My father died two years before I "found" him.

Instead, I found Florine, a treasure, a kindness, his widow. I had, in that spring of 1994, from our small, decrepit cabin on Lopez Island, Washington, summoned nerve and called. A relative of Edgar's, easily tracked down, had provided me with his widow's number in Nebraska. When the phone was answered and I was assured it was she, I asked, "Does the name Phyllis Giammatteo mean anything to you?"

A pause. "I think I know what this phone call is about," a kind voice filled it. And then we were off.

"Ask me anything," she said.

She had known all this time. Before they married, Edgar told her everything. It had been a requirement of the marriage that Florine knew. So they advanced upon their lives together with that knowledge and agreed that if I ever turned up, they would welcome me.

This detail remains the most healing in my passage from lost to found. I was known about. Out there was the warmth and possibility of welcome.

"Come visit," she said. "Come learn more."

"Plus," she added, when we were about to say good-bye, "I'm going to call a family meeting and tell the kids."

The kids. I had sisters. I had brothers. More than one.

⇌

EDGAR NEHEMIAH OSBORNE WAS BORN IN NOVA
Scotia. Florine would flesh out the few facts with anecdotes,
memories, photographs. His mother required herself to be
called only Mrs. Osborne-with-an-"e." She seemed to live independent of a first name. Widowed, she moved with her sons to
New Brunswick, there to work as the housekeeper for a Presby-
terian minister, even though, as I recall, she was Acadian. She
was described as thin-lipped and austere.

Edgar himself was neither. Handsome, a redhead, he was
reported by one daughter to have been funny, warm, kind, an
accessible fellow, quick to rage and quick to forget what enraged
him; to clap you on the shoulder and share a beer. He was
loved, it seemed, for his humor and directness.

Florine loved his red hair. "He hated it," she said. He was
as far away from Dr. Stout as I would prove to be from my
newly acquired half siblings. They'd ended up in Nebraska
because Florine had family there. Nebraska! Let me tell you
where. If you pick up your rental car in Denver, Colorado, you
head south, winding down out of the mountains and boulder
country, onto the plains. You inhabit flatness, becoming a dot
making its way across miles and miles of grid. At a certain
point, you imagine yourself to be in the middle of many things
—the state, the country, the long summer day, the middle of
some journey you can't turn back from but have ceased to
believe has value.

Beaver City, Nebraska, where my father and his family
would end up, is slightly above its border with Kansas—in the
middle. If I drove a tad beyond a barely marked turn on the
endless gravel road, acres and acres of pastures and fields like

quilts spread out in all directions, I would cross the state line. It seemed I did this several times before freeing myself from languor. Finally, I made the correct turn and headed up the road to Beaver City. It was August—hot and humid. In Nebraska, whether near or far, hog farms release astonishingly vile and pervasive pig shit fumes into the ubiquity, and so there was that, heralding my arrival.

I traveled with my journal and a fifth of Johnnie Walker Red.

This is where he ended up—happily, it seemed—with his family of seven. Would I be regarded as the eighth?

As far away from my father as possible, this father, a man who, if five children could be reckoned evidence, savored the life of the body, and familial chaos. For a while, Florine said, he worked as a roustabout. Sounds like something you'd call a dog, or a tavern. A roustabout? Who even really had a job called that? It was sweaty; it was rough around the edges. But then there was Florine—warm gray-blue eyes, thought-provoking books on every table.

Edgar drove a truck after that, owned a rig. At some point, in that capacity, he broke his back—an accident involving a bicyclist and a dark, slick out-of-state road. He smoked and died in his bed of lung cancer. Rough around the edges, this dad. What of him did I carry? I don't know, but it was comforting, all the same, to imagine that the great mismatch between my father Dr. Stout, and me had some origin in what I got from Edgar.

A common man, well loved, albeit with a temper, who loved to work in wood.

⇌

I SEARCHED FLORINE'S COMMEMORATIVE WALL FOR A photograph that might contain something of me in my father's face. Nothing.

"Do I look at all like him?" I asked Florine, while standing in her narrow entryway before the breakfast nook.

"Oddly, no. I see nothing." She shook her head sadly.

Their five children's names all started with a "J." And they all looked like admixtures of both parents, with Florine's features dominating. My sense of exile deepened. The eldest in this family of formerly seven, I felt like a freak in this Nebraska outpost—a single woman, *gay*; dressed in my signature color, *black*; with short hair and pierced ears; there in a prairie home with a parlor, antimacassars armoring the chairs, in the exact middle of . . . *something*. But for the kindness of Florine, I might have bolted.

She produced a sticky note. It was a list Edgar had made to remind himself what to bring Florine when she had been in the hospital many years before: comb, paperback, floss, mints.

I asked, "Did he make a lot of lists?"

"Oh, yes. He was quite compulsive. Endless lists. Here—you can have this one."

I took it, tickled to have proof that I had inherited the list gene, for I, too, am an avid and compulsive maker of lists.

SO—I'VE GOT FOUR PARENT TYPES AND HALF A DOZEN siblings. It is peculiar, in the way of things, and in some contexts not strange at all—after all, it takes a village. How odd, how happy, to find myself so not alone. Four parent-like figures, half a dozen half siblings—two unencountered, four met—and in turn some half dozen of their children. Myriad types of familial configurations make growing up in the petri dish of the American nuclear family *the* peculiar norm.

LOST, TUMBLED, SEEKING, SOUGHT. THERE IS AN ALCHEMY of loss. It combines chance and what you do with it; serendipity; how memory stirs it all to make a self. What brings closure? Is this question even apt? What urges the salubrious pause, the *enough, already,* the shift in perspective, however slight, that generates forgiveness? The details of the narrative cease to matter as the defining things. I tracked down information, *my* information. I believed that once I acquired my heap of facts surrounding the adoption narrative—surrender, placement, search, reunion—meaning would alchemically transpire.

To get, to win, to be given "my" origin story, drivingly important, I had to keep my gaze fixed exclusively on that. But now, however many, many years later, I see it's not the details, nor their falling into a cohesive story, that is the point. It's what the journey has required and subsequently shaped, and how both have illuminated the underpinnings to release them, freeing me to choose presence, to choose to be here now, in the coruscating present.

THIRTEEN

⇌

My *Christian Science*

THE CHURCH OF MY CHILDHOOD WAS A SMALL, DARK
brown log cabin, bordered by a rose garden on one side and a
shallow pool on the other. In deep winter we would ice-skate
there. The cabin exuded old-wood and dusty smells. Thick,
dark curtains offered protection to the worshippers from
whatever daylight held. There were powdery female fragrances
and an amber glow from the lamps that flanked two lecterns.
These functioned as the Christian Science altar, where the
first and second readers read alternately from the Bible and
Science and Health with Key to the Scriptures, by Mary Baker
Eddy, which, in turn, functioned as both the preacher and the
sermon.

I remember a boy with straw-colored hair named Robert.
He was deformed and always cheerful, his face inclined at an
angle as he looked up with glowing, loving eyes from his
wheelchair. His legs were small and shrunken, his chest as
bony and fragile as a bird's. But he would be dressed, every

Sunday, in a crisp white shirt and tie, his doll legs tucked neatly inside pressed trousers.

Unlike the work of most religions, Christian Science sets no place for grief or pain—spiritual, psychological, or physical —at its table. Heartfelt entreaties for the sick and the bereaved are not among the faith's gestures. This is because Mary Baker Eddy and her religion dismissed the physical world in all its manifestations, and thus we saw a perfect Robert, God's lovely little boy, for whom the wheelchair, crutches, and withered limbs were at best illusions, at worst annoyances of a temporary nature, and whose dreams of climbing trees, running with his dog, and making love must be tumbled in Mary Baker Eddy's thought machine, there cleansed of depression, defeat, and despair. Poor Robert found an ample challenge as God's Perfect Child.

Should young Robert, our exemplary Christian Scientist, experience torment of the flesh or mind, he must regard it as a belief that indicates a momentary failure in the sovereign belief of man's perfection. Once corrected, this error, this delusion that the physical has anything truthful to express, will resume its seat, in the back, behind Mind, the driver. Even death, which along with birth constitutes the most physical of physical realities, was banished from Mrs. Eddy's Perfect Plane, believed to be itself a belief. Death represents the failure to clearly comprehend and demonstrate the truths of Christian Science.

What *are* the truths of Christian Science, notwithstanding the paradoxical truth of Mrs. Eddy's death, at ninety, of pneumonia?

I was young when I "practiced" it, and I "understood," foggily and with a child's raw and loyal fervor, God to be synonymous with words—seven synonyms, to be exact, according to Mary Baker Eddy: Life, Truth, Love, Soul, Spirit, Mind, and God. Man was the perfect reflection of these words. Everything else—the material world, head colds and cancer, dark nights of the soul, death—did not exist. Everything else was an illusion to be dispelled and dispersed as if waving your hands through a cloud of gnats or mosquitoes.

In Sunday school, we would recite, with baffling conviction, Mrs. Eddy's "Scientific Statement of Being": "There is no life, truth, intelligence, nor substance in matter. All is infinite Mind and infinite manifestation, for God is All-in-all. Spirit is immortal truth; matter is mortal error. Spirit is the real and eternal; matter is the unreal and temporal. Spirit is God, and man is His image and likeness. Therefore man is not material; he is spiritual."

I did not understand this (who did?), but I was convinced that good would amass through the power of recitation.

I understood that *Science and Health with Key to the Scriptures* was a sacred text, a book equal in spiritual heft to the Bible, although I understood rarely and only then dimly the text's content. It is over seven hundred pages of egregious prose. The first edition, written in 1875, would be followed by 432 revisions. This excruciating labor of a lifetime had less to do with the growing sophistication of Mary Baker Eddy's thought than with her fierce commitment to self-promotion, but who knew? Her book *feels* profound, seeming to promise that if you pore over it sincerely and in a routine manner, you might extract a pearl. But Mrs. Eddy's remains a text not so much thought out and subsequently organized as a stream-of-consciousness exhalation, pickled in lofty aphorisms and brined in delusion. No one picks it up for a joyful canter through it.

Mark Twain suggested that it be translated into English; Harold Bloom identified its prose style as "one of the great ordeals of the American Religion."

On her astonishingly impenetrable, elliptical, and incoherent "prose" style, Twain opined in *Christian Science*:

> Mrs. Eddy has one very curious and interesting peculiarity: whenever she notices that she is chortling along without saying anything, she pulls up with a sudden "God is over us all," or some other sounding irrelevancy, and for the moment it seems to light up the whole district; then, before you can recover from the shock, she goes flitting pleasantly and meaning-lessly along again, and you hurry hopefully after her, thinking you are going to get something this time; but as soon as she has led you far enough away from her turkeylet she takes to a tree. Whenever she discovers that she is getting pretty disconnected, she couples-up with an ostentatious "But" which has nothing to do with anything that went before or is to come after, then she hitches some empties to the train—unrelated verses from the Bible, usually—and steams out of sight and leaves you wondering how she did that clever thing.

My "churched" years—from roughly 1953, when I was five, to 1966, when late adolescence ushered in an atheistic frame of mind—shaped my conviction that church and Sundays, however accompanied by endless boredom and ennui, and God, whose omnipotent ire bade life to pause, were necessary conditions of moral being. I loved *my* Christian Science, its magic and imperious pronouncements. To a child, it could be quite wonderful. All you needed was to think yourself into a perfect relationship with God, and then there would never be sore throats and eczema, Aunt Gaddy's cancer of the jaw, familial disasters, the troubling emergence of pubic hair. Christian Science promulgated Good and banished Evil, bravely denying its existence, so it guaranteed happiness should one's thoughts successfully repel the taint of Error.

But I remember the whispers and hints of dark matters. The smart, elegant first reader, Jeri McCaferty, had a disabled daughter; Isobel Trembley's husband was a drunk; there was Robert in his braces and wheelchair; Matt Gillespi, my piano teacher, had a disconcerting habit of sitting Way Too Close beside me on the bench, sharing the smell of his greasy hair tonic, his warm, yeasty fingers, his stale and furry breath. The dark details had nothing to do, in any spoken way, with Christian Science. But they would emerge in the phone conversations between Isobel and Mother that I overheard occasionally. There was nothing explicit in these calls; only, when they ended, Mother always said, "Isobel is such a complainer," with a particular tone of voice and something tense in her features. And Linda, Mrs. McCaferty's older girl, was not born disabled. She had contracted rheumatic fever when an infant, and the Christian Science intended to heal her had not. She would spend her life an eternal, masturbating, fat twelve-year-old who eventually needed to be institutionalized.

It seemed mostly a world of women, although that cannot have been true. But something about the Christian Science aura—blandly pleasant, somewhat whispery, a little thin-lipped, as if the collective concentration on mind over matter pinched the features—seemed to emasculate or unsex or render gender-neutral the congregation.

My mother loved *her* Christian Science, until she didn't. A midlife hysterectomy severed her connection with the church, whose principles forbade any medical intervention, regardless of the severity of one's physical condition. Betrayed, Mother shifted her loyalties to medicine and had the surgery. No practitioner would hold her in prayer or thought. Years later, she took up the faith again, adding a splash of Pentecostal fun with Oral Roberts, the rich and charismatic televangelist, who preached prosperity and, like Mary Baker Eddy, sanctioned the acquisition of wealth.

Mother relished her prosperity; loved *nice* things; retained an Armenian seamstress, Corinne; cultivated an avidity for antiques and Hummel figurines; pressed all to regard her as a *lady.* Perhaps all this did sit comfortably both with her humble origins and with the true teachings of Christianity—generosity, compassion, simplicity. These were anathema to Christian Science. In her suppression of emotion and the life of the body, something wanted to get through. Mother's hypochondria seemed in dialogue with Christian Science. She sought always to be healed. Oral Roberts, like Mary Baker Eddy, merged prayer and healing. His hospital focused on treating spirit, mind, *and body*, though. Perhaps her faith in him was her way of getting to have, and validate, a body.

She studied her Christian Science daily, following a weekly lesson plan laid out in the *Christian Science Quarterly,* which formed a sort of dialogue between selected passages from the Bible and *Science and Health.* Although these lessons were elusive, I strove to apprehend them. There were intriguing study aids—authentic chalk, periwinkle blue, in a special holder to highlight the weekly passages. Once the weekly lessons were completed, the passages could be erased with a

Christian Science square of chamois, soft and worn. Most thrilling was the set of springy metal braces that fitted onto the books like harness to horse. The numbered tabs coordinated the passages between the Bible and *Science and Health*. Thus equipped, we would *study*.

To this day, I replicate this ritual, gathering my texts, articles, tablet, and pens toward a tidy pile on the table. I like the meaning that such focus, with its lovely props, confers. But when it comes to *thinking*, taking substance from my assembled texts to form and inform thought, I struggle. It's as if I, under Mother's sway, position myself in the intent slump of study without any map of how to think. How do we learn thinking? What is meant by it? Not mind chatter or the narratives created out of feeling states—jealousy; anger—which in turn, spur behavior on. I mean thinking *about* an idea, a piece of history, a paragraph. How in the world does one interact intelligently, reasonably, with this:

> To admit physical effects is to conclude matter cause and effect, whence it follows there are two causes, viz., mind and matter, else that mind produces matter, or matter produces mind, which contradicts the science of Life in its demonstration, and is like saying dust originated man, and a serpent a dove. (*Science and Health*, 1875 edition).

It hurts the brain to wrestle these words even into a semblance of clarity. The best I can do is to imagine a Scientist or a practitioner engaged in an argument with some condition at hand. Let's say I have a headache—but, according to Eddy's "thought," it is not real. My head is the perfect creation of

God and, as such, can experience no pain. Therefore, it is error; some erroneous thought about my true spiritual nature is giving me a headache. I don't need an aspirin; I need a freshly laundered thought. I need to push my tangled thinking inside the Seven Synonyms Machine, tumble it around, and realign. This is, alas, how I learned to "think."

Christian Science prayer is an insistence on perfection, a demand to feel *good* against any evidence of the body as it sojourns in the material world. Emotions are messy—worse, terrifying—and so are subject to somatization, landing in the body, where they must be denied. Direct contact with experience, also terrifying, can be revised by thinking, which is, in turn, perverted by eradicating the truth of matter with a blast of Perfect Mind. You see what a tailspin any healthy mind gets itself in when trying to think logically about Christian Science?

WHY DID THIS BECOME MY MOTHER'S PASSION, THIS indecipherable system that severed mind and thinking from all that is, to the human senses, real? My mother was raised in poverty by an overbearing mother who married three times. She never knew her father, claimed that he had died before her birth. She would reveal very little of the hardships of her childhood. Yet her profound yearning for the love of her mother, and for a physically present father, and for a Perfect Family, suggests a belief that if one could just get one's thinking right, then the world would conform to "perfection."

The phrase "nothing's perfect" seemed to Mother the equivalent of heartbreak. For the Scientist, perfection is a spiritual path, and Mrs. Eddy's folly intersected, I believe, with Mother's mental anguish. Her dream of having a Perfect

Family was upended by her inability to have children, a festering "imperfection" that, thus framed, remained a signature sorrow. "All I ever wanted was . . . ," she would repeat over the years of my growing up. Saying it, she would frame me in her powerfully disappointed gaze. I myself did not constitute a Perfect Family, nor was I its main ingredient. At some point, the present tense changed to the past tense and regret and resentment were added to the roux.

What was she trying to think away? The disconcerting "truth" of imperfection? *All I ever wanted was a Perfect Family.* Did that declaration have its roots in Christian Science? Really, families' imperfections, is the stuff of drama, novels, vibrant human life. If only she could think away the imperfections: the infertility (hers or his); the ordeal of the adoption process (which, she reported tersely to have been an "ordeal"); the occurrence in her life of someone else's child; the abysmal gap between her desire and the ineradicable reality that was I.

I may be dumb myself in this respect, but what is the difference between working the abstract principles of Christian Science and eradicating what is "real"—the tooth's shrill pain because it's actually cracked; the meetings with fear and sorrow? Unaddressed, they are projected outward: You *are the problem; the disappointment.* You *are Error.*

Unsurprisingly, religion became repulsive to me, and yet it was the foundation upon which I had built a kind of ethical vocabulary. Mrs. Eddy's God was unsatisfying, after all—more of a banker than a deity, or a dispenser of treats and comforts. The Eddyan God, those seven dancing words, that blotting-out of pain and unhappiness, made me yearn for the opposite: a God whose mysteries would not be cheapened by the distortion of human will. If God stands in for the human yearning to extract morsels of the divine from the daily stew, then it follows that certain constructions of the divine—kindness, honesty, generosity—must be cultivated. Christian Science, however, contains no system of ethical behavior; what in life is unattractive can be simply thrown away.

Consciously or not, I began to exorcise the Christian Science from my thinking, unintentionally drawn to parallels with the old "new thought" in various New Age romps. My Decade of Dalliances in the 1980s offered up a sampler of psycho-spiritual fads, themselves echoes of Mary Baker Eddy's mid-nineteenth-century fixations—mesmerism, parlor séances, utopianism, phrenology, the laying-on of hands. With my twentieth-century group of spiritually inclined friends, I studied the Seth Material and attended many channeled "lectures"; tallied and vigorously transformed our psycho-spiritual challenges through the number systems of the Enneagram; participated in workshops led by an enigmatic figure named Mitzie, who "taught" us how to breathe. I even went to a psychic, or a channeler (I don't know who is called what anymore), who officiated in a trailer park off tawdry, sordid Aurora Avenue and received wisdom and stories tailored to the queries of her customers from a prophet called Jeremiah. Jeremiah advised me to, when emotionally wrought, wear pastel-colored clothing.

These were the children of Christian Science. There seemed not much distance between the spiritual fads of Mary Baker Eddy's epoch and the New Age foolishness of ours: folly, and constant wardrobe changes.

Still shopping for spiritual gratification, I became a Catholic for a little while. This yearning followed the eight-month peace walk I took. We met many ardent Catholics along the way—nuns, mostly, committed to social justice. Some walked with us; some sponsored the walk; all worked tirelessly for justice and the brave application of Christian values. Some had broken with the church in order to continue their work, which was too progressive for Rome. These women —sweet-voiced, sturdy, committed to the Good—filled me with awe and envy, and partly inspired my stop at the Benedictine monastery for solitude and healing.

Back home in Seattle, with trepidation and a deep sense of unworthiness, I asked for preliminary instruction from the Catholics. This was catechism class, a rich and forbidden-sounding term, where I hoped in a week to be filled with the ideas and the language of Thomas Merton, Henri Nouwen, David Steindl-Rast—those Christian philosophers who had, in spirit, accompanied us on the peace walk. It soon became clear that the catechism class was a kind of simplistic indoc-trination, and I remembered ruefully that my nuns, whom I held in such esteem, had themselves repudiated Catholic dogma. I could not go on, but this disappointment didn't stanch yearning.

Buddhism would become my spiritual practice, offering techniques and perspectives that inspired a vigorous and layered exploration of life. In contrast with the prescribed denial and disembodiment of Christian Science, the Buddhist commits to exploring what is real. *Get down, smell it, roll around* might be construed as the instruction. Only by ex-ploring mental states deeply, as many as one hosts, in all their variations—frightened, craving, drenched in joy—and by approaching all there is with curiosity and acceptance can a mind become free and truly happy.

I've practiced Buddhism for over thirty years, packing

myself off to retreats, studying with and without groups and teachers, attending lectures. I have always thought this a practical, if difficult, spiritual path, leading one toward an intimate relationship with oneself and a generosity in dealing with others. The path cultivates wisdom and compassion in this world—a precious antidote to Mrs. Eddy's disembodied hooey. But *my* Christian Science predisposed me to an interest in Buddhist practice, I believe. It made me well versed in mind over matter and magical faith in the power of visualization and any number of affirmations that tout the power of the mind to shape reality, and thus *my* Buddhism followed on the heels of these experiments, all huddling under the umbrella of the New Age. And as I scroll back through the highlights of my spiritual love affairs—a two-year stint with the macrobiotics in Boston, serial joinings with diverse Buddhist groups, the foray into Catholicism—I wonder now whether *my* Buddhism is laced with a legacy left me by Christian Science, whether *my* Buddhism is Christian Science transposed.

MARY BAKER EDDY WAS BORN ON JULY 16, 1821, A RICH and steamy time for American religion. Mormonism had been handed to Joseph Smith a few miles up the road, *The Book of Mormon* "revealed" in 1830. Seventh-Day Adventism was unloosing its end-of-the-world predictions upon the firmament. The message was clear: anyone could create, discover, found, or channel a religion.

Many avenues of charlatanism and spiritualism made themselves available to Mary Baker Eddy; she began her career as a clairvoyant, presiding over séances as a medium. Enamored of herself, she indulged in writing verse, frequently publishing in the local newspaper. That slim fame emboldened her to introduce herself as an "authoress," but, as Willa Cather, writing for *McClure's* magazine in the early 1900s, noted, Eddy's writings indicated "her difficulties with punctuation, which was always a laborious second thought with her. From her letters and early manuscripts it is evident that lucid, clean-cut expression was almost impossible. . . . Her mind was as untrained as her pen."

I alight with chagrin and revulsion on the detail of Mary Baker Eddy's appropriation of motherhood. She elevated its sublimity while rejecting the actual role. Unable to tolerate her little boy, George, she farmed him out to relatives. Finally, the housekeeper adopted George, with Mary's agreement. They departed for Minnesota, thus leaving Mary, in her distorted view, abandoned. Seeking solace, she ordered the construction of a cradle, in which she slept, paying her relatives to rock her.

In a perversion of primal need, Mary Baker Eddy would come to idealize the image of the mother, embracing it as central in the representation of her church and her leadership. Hers was the Mother Church; she penned a hymn called "Mother's Evening Prayer"; her exclusive room in the Mother Church was Mother's Room. In her autobiography, *Retrospection and Introspection*, she wrote, "The true mother never willingly neglects her children in their early and sacred hours, consigning them to the care of nurse or stranger. Who can feel and comprehend the needs of her babe like the ardent mother?"

Mary Baker Eddy was less the "discoverer" of Christian Science than its plagiarist. The beliefs that constituted *her* Christian Science were lifted from the works of Phineas Parkhurst Quimby, her mentor in the new mind science. In the first edition of *Science and Health* (1875), she credited Quimby, but as Mrs. Eddy's reputation as teacher and founder grew, she distanced herself from her old mentor, finally claiming that it was she who had instructed and inspired him.

Traces of established philosophical thought waft through Mrs. Eddy's work, although, read in the context of the times, the whole remains a hodgepodge. Jonathan Edwards's Calvinist perfectionism, Benjamin Franklin's pragmatism, Transcendentalism and Emersonian self-reliance strut and cross the Christian Science stage. She continued to pilfer here and there, taking a few key points from the Shakers, also flourishing in that part of New England. As would be true for Mrs. Eddy, the Shakers were frequently in and out of court, disputing laws created to destroy their scandalous practices. Ann Lee, the founder, believed herself to be the female Christ; Mary Baker Eddy followed suit. Ann Lee asked her followers to call her Mother; Mary Baker Eddy thought that was a fine idea and applied it to herself. Both women embraced celibacy; indeed, Mary Baker Eddy thought that sex was and would become universally unnecessary. At a future time, when all evolved beings would have become Christian Scientists, reproduction would occur from thought and babies would be born from "mental generation." The following appeared in the 1886 edition of *Science and Health*:

The propagation of their species without the male element, by butterfly, bee, and moth is a discovery corroborative of the Science of Mind, because it shows that the origin and continuance of these insects rest on Principle, apart from material conditions. An egg never was the origin of a man, and no seed ever produced a plant . . . the belief that life can be in matter, or soul in body, and that man springs from dust or from an egg, is the brief record of mortal error . . . The plant grows not because of seed or soil.

Christian Science made you think you should be above it all; that if your thoughts were purely pure, which is to say, in refutation of physical reality, you would receive money, radiant health, and happiness. *Obey me, and these shall follow,* Mrs. Eddy all but said. In the mid–nineteenth century, her religion piggybacked onto the dawning awareness of the powerful machinery of the mind, to which Mary Baker Eddy added her vibrant paranoia, naming all imagined slights, criticisms, and threats to *her* Christian Science malicious animal magnetism, or MAM! Always uttered with an exclamation point, MAM! permeated Eddy's teachings, the lives of her students, and even the continuously revised *Science and Health*. She was crazed by it—nothing was free from its influence—yet it remained a remarkably convenient fabrication. If Mrs. Eddy was accused of treachery or slander, she blamed MAM! If any of her followers doubted the pervasive influence of mesmerism, he or she was said to be under its very influence and was banished.

I wonder if my Christian Science–besotted mother believed in the fact and ubiquity of MAM! Ever wary of my coercion by evil influences, she did not know that she herself had fallen for those very things she feared on my behalf. In a religion so laced with the eccentricities, fears, and scrambled thinking of the founder, why judge? In my pursuit of spiritual teachings, it was not at all uncommon for this guru or that great teacher to be embroiled in some sexual scandal, or two. Charisma and its kissing cousin, abuse of power, seem prime ingredients in the dish of a new faith and its subsequent success or failure.

The philosophical vagaries of Christian Science, themselves in their day an amalgam of the new "American thought," have fueled myriad movements of the present. To the then-growing popularity of "mind science," Mrs. Eddy stapled her notion of religion, seeing in the marriage the potential for great financial gain. Mark Twain relished his dissections of the Eddy phenomenon. His caustic, witty attack on Christian Science and its founder was triggered by his fear, in 1898, that the cult would spread so rapidly that it would control Congress by the 1930s. At the turn of the twentieth century, the religion had grown at an astonishing rate. He credited Mary Baker Eddy's business savvy for protecting Christian Science from the fate typically reserved for cults, and her genius for mammon for engendering the success of the political and financial machinery of the church.

IT SEEMS TO ME PECULIARLY AMERICAN, THIS INVENtion and reinvention of a singular, self-promoting self that pulls strands of ill-digested philosophical ramblings and raw sentimentality from a disordered mind, matches them to the fears and hopes of a particular public, fabricates a sect, and whips up a following. Mary Baker Eddy, having gained enormous fame in the promulgation of *her* Christian Science, reigned over it with tyrannical vigilance. Where in many sects the muscular, passionate, ever-evolving argument with God and faith is key to the religion's evolution, Mrs. Eddy's Christian Science squelched all questioning. Alarmed that any thinking outside her system would dethrone her, she issued strict rules declaring that no material on mental healing other than hers be made available to students or to her cohort of teachers. She forbade any original preaching on or interpreting of her text, naming the texts themselves as preachers. "This service," Mrs. Eddy declared, "was 'authorized' by Christ."

Mother studied, did her homework, plodded on. Now I repeat the ritual. Mine is not a study of Mrs. Eddy's text. Rather, I read *about* the founder, seeking to understand how the swirling, convoluted, oracular Christian Science shaped my mind, by learning something of its context and history.

When asked, Mother would not comment on what, in *her* Christian Science, she was reading. Instead, she'd say, "I do not discuss *my* Christian Science," or she might read a passage out loud and then say innocently, "We'll ask your father later."

Why do I fuss? Mother's advocacy of a religion she claimed to love but never understood seemed as dumb as it did stubborn. Raising to a virtue the disregard of somatic life, of emotions and of critical thinking allowed her to remain psychologically incurious. In other words, it shut the door on me.

Much occurred between us to strain and fray our love, tumbled, as she insisted, in the drum of Mrs. Eddy's thought machine. But nothing would be quite so permanently sundering as the strange case of Mother's knee.

FOURTEEEN

⇌

The Strange Case of Mother's Knee

A FEW YEARS AFTER I CHANGED MY STOUT NAME TO the name I thought of as a flower, and after I'd found and met the Other Mother, Phyllis, and after, finally, the churlish power afforded by withholding the information from the Stouts subsided and the desire to share began, I asked Mother to visit me, by herself, in Seattle. She agreed, and I made a plan for what I hoped would be a mutually conciliatory and cathartic stay. And so I booked a room at a charming Victorian resort on the Saanich Peninsula in British Columbia, noted for its spectacular location, quiet charm, and lovely food, replete with vegetables and flowers from its garden. I imagined the intimate disclosure of my reunion experience with Phyllis, and the fact that I had decided to take back the name she had, at birth, given me. I imagined Mother's interest and curiosity, against all evidence our history offered. Was I being sadistic? Oblivious to the suffering I would cause her? In retrospect, I would frame it thus:

I lured my mother west and, once I had her there, further kidnapped her to Canada, where I proceeded to bludgeon her with Truth.

IT WAS AUTUMN. ON THE DAY OF OUR ARRIVAL, THE SUN had broken through the clouds, collapsed in purple heaps low on the horizon. Whiffin Spit, a strip of pebbly land twenty feet wide and half a mile long, projected into the water, creating eddies and swirls. A lush garden surrounded the main lodge. Flowers and herbs tilted against one another from a cacophony of heights. Low, creeping thymes and rosemary encroached pleasantly on nasturtiums and pansies. The breeze blew cool and briny, and fragrances of sun-warmed herbs and broth and roasting garlic wafted from the open kitchen door.

"I hope we're in time for lunch," said Mother. It was the first thing she'd said in hours.

I would make the First Terrible Disclosure over tea in the atrium of the Four Seasons hotel in Seattle. "I've planned a little trip for us, Mom," I said, leading up to it.

"I'm on a trip," she said.

"I thought it would be fun to see some of the country," I said.

"A bus tour of the city?"

"No, Mom. Canada," I said.

She buttered her roll with concentration. She always had an uncanny ability to know when something was up. Here I was, coaxing her to abandon all the things she loved and trusted—the elegant hotel, the anticipation of exquisite dinners, shopping—and head out to a strange, wild island, where I planned to throw all that had been avoided, all that had never been discussed, into her face. In that context, was there even a possibility of right timing? I could not keep postponing the telling that I'd changed my name. I'd made our Sooke reservations in that name, and she'd find out sooner or later.

"I have another name," I blurted, stirring a glob of honey in my tea. "I don't know if you ever knew that. My name before you named me." My heart was pounding.

"I'm going to collect these wonderful little honeys for you. They're such a convenience when traveling," Mother said, and reached for my jar and popped it into her bag.

I looked directly at my mother. "I have taken my birth name. I'd like to tell you about that." I had thought only cursorily about how to break the news; anxiety and desire had overwhelmed thinking. I suspected that one made this kind of disclosure in increments, dropping a pellet here, a pellet there, accreting to a patty of information. "I changed my name to Hollis—*back* to Hollis, that is. It was the name I started out with," I said. And what did I want Mother to call me in the best of all possible worlds? Nor had I thought through that.

She paused, as if trying to stir my new-old name into her cup of tea. "Why in the world?" she faltered. "I don't understand."

"It's my name," I said. "My birth name. The name on my birth certificate."

"Not the one we have," she said in an underlining fashion. Something like a hook drew the corners of Mother's mouth, tugging and letting go, tugging and letting go. She replaced the cup in its saucer and stared at the far wall across the twinkling room.

⇌

I could not know what Mother took in from our talk at tea. Out onto the spit, she wobbled in her heels. Its center mounded and unnavigable, it was dense with salal, heaps of fallen logs, their twisting branches weathered to stubs. Way out at sea, a freighter looked determined and rusty and emboldened the line drawn by the horizon.

"When we go back inside to register, you will hear that name again," I said. "I made our reservation in that Hollis name. I don't want it to catch you off guard."

"The flowers are so beautiful in their garden," Mother said. "We really must ask for a tour."

"Great," I said.

The concierge's desk, high and dark, reminded me of a confessional. I said my name, enunciating carefully, aiming my words at the face of the concierge, forming them as if my name were an outstanding wine that I was recommending. The concierge arranged her piles of paper.

Mother stood stiffly beside me. "Are we late for lunch?" she asked.

"Your name again?" asked the concierge.

"Stout," my mother said, as I said, simultaneously, "Giammatteo." Suddenly, I knew I had condemned myself to a lifetime of endless spellings and repetitions and subsequent blank stares. I looked at Mother and Mother looked at me as if we were in separate parties. My chest felt like a little girl's— all rib cage, a small barrel without breasts. My lungs and ribs ached with the strain of breathing. In her presence, I had said it several times out loud, my new-old name, but for the first time, she "got" it. Absolutely still, as if on the guided tour already, arms in front joined at the wrist, her purse perfectly centered, she held herself carefully intact.

"I'll take our stuff upstairs and meet you in the dining room." I said, and bolted.

I was unnerved by my mother's absolute resistance to meaningful exchanges. I studied the spit from the small dormer in our shared room. The sky was big and many shades of gray. I regretted not having my own room.

"It wasn't my intention to hurt you, Mom," I said in the airy dining room.

"What kind of name is that?" she asked, buttering a roll with care.

"Italian," I said. "The last name, anyway."

"I should have seen this coming," Mother snapped, no pause between the expression of curiosity and rage. "It is absolutely tragic." Her expression remained masklike.

"What is?" I asked.

"Your behavior; your behavior is. You have done this deliberately to hurt us," Mother said, and dropped her voice to a whisper sibilant with hatred. "We gave you so much. We wanted the best for you."

I excused myself and bolted again, heading for the river.

There was odd splashing there, and a slice of red cut through the white spray. There was the smell of dying. Ten feet away, the water split; salmon were thrashing in pools so shallow that their dorsal fins broke through. They were turning red as they were dying. Carcasses dotted the bank, some half out of water, some floating, snouts breaking the surface. Some of the dead darkened the greeny bottom like shadows. Five hung suspended in the water. Strips of their flesh hung off them, and there were gouges in their muscular sides. The mottled red skin exploded in places to a deep maroon. They hung wide-eyed, mouths agape. I wondered if, in my human life, there would be such a moment when, perfectly spent, because of perfectly performing my one appointed task, I, too, could hang in a clear green medium, eyes bright circles, mouth drinking in the sweetness of closure. But it was time to get back to Mother and assess the damage.

In our tiny room, she was studying *her* Christian Science. "What are you reading?" I asked, knowing the answer.

"I don't share *my* Christian Science," Mother said.

"It's not like I don't know," I said. "I grew up with it."

"I don't share *my* Christian Science," she repeated. "It is between Jesus and me."

"I didn't know you had a *personal* relationship with Jesus," I said testily.

"I love him. He loves me," she said, and, after a small silence, "hand me the afghan, please. I can't get it."

"How come?" I asked.

"I injured my knee," she said. "I shouldn't have gone on that walk. The ground was too uneven."

I struggled to bring into focus the culprit twig, the errant pebble, waiting on the vile and treacherous spit to upend her.

Tucking herself in, she remounded her piles of Christian Science on both sides of her knees. "I'm afraid I'll have to call your father," she said. "I already called Mrs. Wentworth. She wasn't in, but she'll call back as soon as she is able."

Mrs. Wentworth, a Christian Scientist practitioner, was the deus ex machina of Mother's life. Admittedly, as a practitioner she was unusual—earthy, humane, willing to ply her faith and, should it prove insubstantial, close the books and call in the physicians. Mother turned a page.

I looked out the window to the spit, where two dogs played, a Black Lab and a Collie. The Lab bounded, loose-lipped and grinning, as the Collie sidestepped daintily. Suddenly, their attention dropped from each other and both turned to run full speed toward the central mound, where a blue heron lifted, its twiggy legs pumping stiffly. Their barking drifted through the open window. I couldn't follow my mother's mind. It was the dogs lunging at each other one minute, the next peeling out and running side by side. My mind felt like a crystal vase, the sides of which were sheer and slippery, so that I found no toehold up and out of my confusion.

"I'm waiting for a call," my mother said. "Mrs. Irene Wentworth is going to call."

I approached her, aching for connection. Was there a way to salvage our time together? Guilty for disappointing Mother, I said, "I didn't mean to hurt you. I did it for myself. All my life—"

She cut me off. "*All your life,*" she repeated in a mocking tone, "all you've ever done is hurt me, push me away, both your father and me. This is just one more thing to make us feel like damn fools."

Reason fled, as did hope for repair. "But you know I've always wanted to know where I came from," I countered. "This has always freaked you out."

"You're right, I haven't understood," she said. "We wanted a perfect little baby. We loved you, and everything we did, you poisoned. It is of the devil," my mother said, her voice rising. "Of the devil," she said again.

I thought if I'd really made a pact with the devil, I'd have negotiated a better deal—a bigger apartment, a Porsche, poems published in *The New Yorker*. I was stunned to realize that she wasn't joking.

"Devil, Devil, be cast out!" she cried, lifting her arm and

pointing her finger from the center of her Christian Science mound. Heavy pellets of rain began to strike the window.

"Oh, Mother, for heaven's sake," I said. "You can't reduce this to such fundamentalist crap. 'Of the devil'?" My rage built. "Fuck you," I said. It was out before I knew it. I said it again. The phone rang. I grabbed a towel. A bath would calm me. I had never said "fuck you" to my mother. There was no way to undo that. Definitely not a Right Speech moment.

Any strong emotions always required a Mrs. Wentworth-ish intervention. Conflicts always landed in Mother's body. I knew that "fuck you" would also find a nerve, a willing organ, a volunteer bone.

IN MY ENVELOPING, LAVENDER-SCENTED BATH, I IMA-gined their Christian Science session:

"Well, Mrs. Wentworth, my daughter's really done it now. As you know, our relationship has never been easy."

"Now, if I recall, Elizabeth, all you ever wanted was a Perfect Family."

Pleased that Mrs. Irene Wentworth had retained the key, Mother would sigh and smile and Mrs. Wentworth would echo it with a deep, fully realized Christian Science sigh. "Tell me, Elizabeth, how can I be of use?"

"She's broken my heart. She's changed the name we gave her, Elizabeth Ann Stout, to some dumb, horrible immigrant name that she claims her seed mother gave her."

"Her what?"

"Her seed mother. Well, it's just about the biggest slap in the face, and I can't understand it."

"Have you eaten?"

"No. I fell down."

"Actually fell? When? Where?"

"No, not actually. I twisted my knee, and I must be very, very careful, Irene."

"Yes, of course. At our age. Knees. Is that what we'll be working on, then?" she might ask in her earthy drawl.

"No. My daughter. I want you to work on her."

"How so, Elizabeth?"

"Well, change her name back, for heaven's sake."

A long pause, not necessarily a Christian Science one, a pause in which would be sought patience, forbearance, bearings themselves, perhaps. "Elizabeth," Mrs. Wentworth would implore, "one cannot ask God to change someone else's behavior. That's not how it works."

"How, then?"

"We could go back to knees."

"I'm sitting with my legs up," Mother might say brightly, glowing in the warmth of Mrs. Wentworth's kind regard.

"Have you rubbed them?"

"No. I called you."

A sigh. "Elizabeth, rub your knees. They are your knees. They are not rentals."

And Mother might begin, with tender fingertips, to massage her knees.

"How is that?" Mrs. Wentworth might ask after a medicinal pause.

"Better—yes, better," Mother might whisper. "I appreciate your help so much, Irene."

"Elizabeth, I've told you before, you must work on recognizing when you need divine guidance and when you need a simple rub. Keep rubbing. Now, talk to me about your daughter."

And Mother would pour out the sordid tale of my stubborn misery, because of the adoption; the ceaseless badgering for information that Mother did not have; and, finally, what she had learned in increments—that I had gotten my original birth certificate in which appeared my original name and God knows what else, and, worse, had started calling myself by this horrid name.

"Where in the world are you, Elizabeth?" Mrs. Wentworth would think to ask.

"She has brought me to this island in Canada. In the middle of nowhere, damp."

"Camping, are you?"

"Oh, no, not camping. We are at an inn."

"How's the food?" Mrs. Wentworth, a gourmet cook herself, would ask.

"Lunch was quite lovely," Mother would say. "Evidentially, the chef is quite well known. They cook with flowers."

"Really, actually cook?"

"I think it would be more accurate to say 'garnish.' Pansies, wonderful herbs." Mother would pronounce the "h."

"So, you're not exactly in the middle of nowhere, then."

"Vancouver Island. She's brought me to a damp place and created a terrible scene."

WE SAT DOWN TO DINNER IN A ROOM SOLEMN AS CHURCH. There's nothing to make one feel so pinned to the wall as public dining following a fight. At least we had our wine. Borage flowers floated like blue stars among the loose petals of calendula in a beautiful, autumnal soup.

"Where are all these people from?" Mother asked. "Are

they from Canada, *Liz*?" The "z's" sounded endless, like a dentist's drill. I was afraid that her astonishing lack of curiosity was genuine and unwooable. My mother was capable of enormous quantities of minutia, bubbling vats of it, endless, empty questions that pertained to nothing of our time together. How could I possibly know where these guests—pale, whispering, polite—came from?

"Yes," I whispered conspiratorially. "Yes."

"Yes, what, sweetie?" my mother asked.

"Yes," I hissed, "they are all from Canada."

"Well, isn't that interesting?" she replied. "Are we close to Alaska?"

I tore my dinner roll.

"I wonder who lives there, in Alaska," she persevered. "Are there Esquimaux?"

"I don't know," I said, after a significant inhalation of wine.

"Are they happy?" She looked with crazed sincerity into my eyes.

"Happy? Well, how would I know?" I asked impatiently. "I do remember reading once that 'Esquimaux' the word is an insult in their language. It means 'fat eaters' or something."

"Well, I certainly don't want to insult them," my mother said, and dipped her spoon into the rich orange soup. "Do they have a university for Esquimaux?"

If my father had been with us, he would have happily assumed the role of Expert that Mother assigned him and would simply have answered, with authority, this idiotic question and all of those to follow, about which he, too, would know nothing.

"I don't want to talk about Esquimaux," I said, and chewed a bitter green, swallowing it whole, throwing wine down after.

"I would like to tell you about finding my birth mother. I met her, Mom," I said, trying to compose myself for her reaction. I went red in the face, and red under my collar, and red inside my heart.

"You met . . . *her*?" Mother asked flatly, pausing between the verb and the object, as if to speak the pronoun might induce the woman to appear.

"Yes, I did. And what I really want to tell you about meeting . . . *her* . . . is how much it made me realize my love for you. That's what I wanted to tell you. It was like a gift, meeting her, if only for that."

Mother seemed to absorb this. "What is she like?" she asked.

I picked at the edges of sundry details—hair, earlobe, polyester pants. I opened my mouth to push out a detail but couldn't. It felt sacrificial, an offering-up of Phyllis on the altar of my mother's rage, albeit momentarily assuaged. I did not trust my mother. Maybe hers was an Esquimaux-type question designed to gain her time, to buy her distance from which she might turn and, weapon reloaded, fire. "She's short," I said, "and doesn't seem very happy."

"Happy," Mother repeated. "What does she do?"

I felt protective of Phyllis. This surprised me. I imagined the disparaging picture painted by the adoption agency and social workers—of a lower class, undereducated, morally slack, out-of-wedlock mother. The words began to snake around our table—the salt and pepper shakers, the hand-painted Italian candleholders, the basket of fresh rolls—"slovenly," "lower-class," "illiterate," "WOP."

"We only just met," I said. "We visited only a little. She moved from Connecticut to California, and then up to Salem,

Oregon, and not much seems to have gone her way." My voice sounded nasal, tinny.

Suddenly, Mother slapped her hand on the table, as if squashing one of the ugly words. "I knew she was a complainer," she said, smirking. "I knew she would be."

"You never met her," I said, incredulous, and closed myself up like a zipper, fearing another "fuck you" leakage.

"If anyone were to ask me about adoption, I'd say it's all a mistake, a terrible mistake," Mother said, swept up in a cold fury. "I don't believe in it any longer. It just causes unhappiness and grief. Look at all we've done for you. We've paid the bills, we've taken the brunt, and you go and hand your life to this bitch on a silver platter."

We sat, stunned, as if looking over a field of debris after a tornado, the losses irreparable, tragic. We were staring hard at each other. Everything there was to say was bound to fall into this miasma of misunderstanding. My mouth made some effort anyway.

"If you say one word," she said, "I will get up and I will leave."

"You're not going to let me respond," I said. It was less a question than an observation.

"I mean it," Mother said to the quivering O my mouth was making.

"I'm sorry. Please," I said. She rose. Our dinners came, and Mother left the table.

She fumbled with a phone book in the lobby. "I'm going to call a cab," she said. "And then I'm going to return to Seattle, and then I'm flying home."

"Mom, please don't go," I said, rubbing my eyes hard. "I'm sorry."

"This is terrible. Terrible," Mother said, and I lunged for her arm. She flinched, and her purse flew off and hit the floor, its contents rolling and fluttering around our feet. Her coin purse burst open. She knelt, scrambling frantically for coins, comb, lipstick, mirror, as if blind. Filled with pity, I joined her on the floor. It was unbearable to see my mother so broken. I'd wanted to explain that I had been flooded with love after finding Phyllis—love for her and Pop, for our struggling unit of a family. It had seemed so right to want to share this. How could something so right have ended up so broken?

She got herself up, snapped her purse shut, and walked up the stairs. I stood, trembling at the bottom. "When my mother left me," I whispered to myself, for I knew that whenever I'd tell this story, that would be how I'd start. In my heart, it would always sound that way.

I imagined the same horrible refrain in my mother's heart: *My daughter is no longer. That is how is has to be. Elizabeth is dead. I have lost my daughter.*

FIFTEEN

⇌

The Claudication of John

I STOOD AWASH IN SUNLIGHT AT JOHN'S DOOR. I knocked and knocked again. Finally, he answered. "Thank you," he shouted, tossing me his usual salad of confused salutations. Since the kiss, he always held my hand a little longer.

"What would you think about taking a walk in the arboretum?" I asked, unable to bear one more pointless trip to Safeway and Bartell.

"Oh, yes, let's," he said enthusiastically. "I've been waiting for you all day."

"But it's only noon," I said.

"Ah, maybe that was yesterday I waited. 'Hollis is coming.' That's what I wrote in my diary, over and over. 'Hollis is coming.' That is all I write anymore. That is so pathetic."

"I think it's sweet," I said. "Uneventful, inaccurate, but very sweet."

I believed that an outing in nature would cheer us. Here, after all, was a man—if his accounts could be believed—who had created garden terraces, curving walkways, and herbaceous borders in a once problematically sloping chunk of yard. Here was a man who possessed the most magnificent magnolia tree I had ever seen. Its trunk was as big around as a man's middle, as tall as the first story of the house. Now in full bloom, John's magnolia hefted a ton of blossoms up to the sky in a frenzied offering. When I walked beneath its canopy on a blue-sky day like this, it took my breath away. The plump and upright petals looked like hands positioned for prayer. They collected into a pink chorale.

And so, with lifted spirits, we agreed to make our way, this day, through nature. A hyacinth sweetness peppered the air. He laughed his first-hour-of-the-visit laugh, hopeful and excited, as if this day might constitute a whole fresh start before, inevitably, he'd turn to me in his last-hour-of-the-day sorrow with the recognition that he was so feeble, usually reported in a stunned tone pierced slightly with revulsion. But his pure eagerness to be off waylaid the gloomy recognition. We shuffled to the car. He stooped, as he did every week, to note the single row of lavender, cup-shaped flowers, and asked, "Do you know what they are called?" to which every week I replied, "Canterbury bells," and slowly, *slowly*, he would bend down to confirm the identification.

THE ARBORETUM REACHED, I PARKED IN A SHADY PULL-off and walked around the car to haul him up and out. He had grown increasingly unable to extricate himself without help, and I was uncertain about how far he was capable of walking. He had a habit of stopping dead in our tracks mid-thought, midsentence, apropos of nothing, an ambulatory non sequitur.

Explaining his stuttered gait, he stopped. "Claudication," he said. "A condition named after Claudius I, emperor of Rome, because, because . . . oh, I don't know. Sometime after the murder of Caligula."

Even his afflictions had their roots in the classics.

The cherry trees were blooming in an overstated way, launching an abundance of blossoms in all directions—vertical and horizontal, arching upward, swooping low. They embodied every kind of movement and every kind of pink, from the subtlest berry hue at the margins to the hysteria of fuchsia. We walked down a long grass corridor flanked by the cherry trees. John stopped, looking down the promenade, struggling with or in a thought, and then began: "Loveliest of trees, the cherry now is hung with . . . with . . ." He began again, slowly reaching up to take the tissue pink between his thumb and finger, while reciting, "Is hung with bloom along the bough," and then he looked at me as if we might spread our wings or, at the very least, our blanket, and sit ourselves among the savories and delights sprung from a picnic basket all graced with a bottle of chilled white wine. As I told you, with the kiss, I should have known better, but I couldn't bring myself to smother our affection. Our fondness for each other was a sad mix—infirmity and imminent good-bye, proxy, shards of memory.

The lane was muddy. The grassy promenade formed a catchment for winter rains draining from the hill. Our feet made sloppy, sucking noises. Against the fabulous pinks, the sky stretched backward up the hill, held aloft by monumental cedars. Farther down the tree-lined corridor, the gardeners had stripped off their rubber overalls and anoraks, as they widened the path to improve the drainage. Even though you would think it the nicest thing in the world to be troweling and scooping and tamping the fragrant earth, they looked sour.

And then, in the middle of all this life and all these sensations, it was time to go. John's energy had left him. "Let's go back," he said.

"Are you all right?" I asked.

He waved the question off him like a bug. "Yes, yes. I want to go home, though." I took his arm and quashed my urge to chat away his grumpiness and my guilt that I may have hauled him out beyond his capabilities. In silence we threaded our way uphill on the narrow path leading to the road.

"You know, *if* you would *use* your cane . . . ," I said

"No, no, no," he said testily.

"Yes," I said. "It would stabilize us. It would make it easier for me."

He looked at me as if I was telling a joke, about to launch into the punch line.

"What are you laughing at?" I asked. "Think of me. Look at me, hauling you all over the place," I said.

"All right," he said. "I shall use the cane."

HE WAS MUTTERING THE FIRST FEW LINES OF THE Housman poem as we entered the house, and had become fixated on the whereabouts of his old college anthology. He wanted to find it so that he could read the thing entire. I figured he'd forget about it soon enough and carried the groceries into the kitchen. I dug the five bags of elbow macaroni from the bottom of the bag. I noted the half-consumed tumbler of vile and tepid French Colombard on the counter.

It alarmed me how John's handsome face one moment

contained all of him, alert and present, and the next collapsed into a mask—an exhausted John; no one there. It seemed sad to leave him at the height of such a brilliant April afternoon. Would he slowly climb the stairs, fording the heavy silence of his big house? Would he sink into his Dim Corner and submit to marathon, mind-numbing TV? Would he think to eat?

He came into the kitchen, book in hand. "I remembered where it was," he said, brandishing an ancient text, fat, black, reminiscent of English classes so far back in time as to summon the moldering smell of brittle paper further compromised by storage. "Come," he said, and led me to the living room. Sunshine was pouring through the French doors at the far end. In the distance, Portage Bay made manifest a perfect urban moment. Pleasure boats sailed its length, between Lake Union and Puget Sound, and blades of light bounced off their bright hulls and swollen, dazzling sails. He turned to me, holding out the book.

"No, you read it," I said.

"Ah, I'm no good at reading poetry out loud," he said.

But I wanted to hear him read the poem in his beautiful, sonorous voice, so courtly and old fashioned. He began to read:

Loveliest of trees, the cherry now
Is hung with bloom along the bough,
And stands about the woodland ride
Wearing white for Eastertide.

Now, of my threescore years and ten,
Twenty will not come again,
and take from seventy springs a score,
It only leaves me fifty more.
And since to look at things in bloom . . .

He paused and looked up. "Do you like the poem?" he asked.

Something in my expression made him think that I was disappointed. More likely, I fought to mask any trace of sadness, the moment poignant and undefended. Astounding, like erupting with song and dance on your way to the corner store, only sad, sad. He sighed and said that it was time to go.

What would he do now? There is just no asking someone who is eighty-six, who can barely walk, who certainly should in no circumstances drive a car, and who is in and out of being aware that his mind is going, "Do you have plans for the evening?" The question feels sadistic.

Guilty and relieved, I walked out into the brilliant afternoon.

I WENT TO SEE JOHN FOR THE LAST TIME IN AUTUMN, which meant that I'd been with him for one year. There were plenty of reasons to stop seeing him. There was the Unfortunate Kiss. There were his bones, whose fragility made our outings strenuous for both of us. The simple placement of limbs had ceased to be a familiar component of his body's language. I believed his decline to be accelerating in proportion to his isolation, but his daughters still could not convince him to move out of the impossible house and into an assisted-living facility.

He was waiting in the vestibule, his beret tipped and rakish. He broke into a delighted smile and grabbed my face. Well, "grab" is a bit overstated, but that's how it felt. He wanted to cradle my face between his warm, dry hands and draw it close to his mouth, with its awakened hunger. I don't know why I couldn't just say, "Now, look, John, I am not your love. I am not your wife. Quit grabbing." But I couldn't bring myself to address the indiscretion.

I took a couple of steps back, demonstrating the requirement of distance, and pointed to his hat. "Time to go," I said. We went, as usual, to Starbucks, and I proceeded to keep not saying, "This is our last time together."

Slowly, he peeled off his coat but forgot to remove his beret. When I got back to our table, bearing coffee, he was squinting at the long wall, a panel of sketches depicting literary luminaries from Jane Austen down the alphabet to Whitman.

"My God, who are those people?" he asked, as if Hitler and his henchmen had just arrived for lunch. "I do not know them," he said testily, shaking his head.

"You do," I contradicted, as we would review *these* characters painted on *this* wall each time we came here, which had amounted to almost every week. "Look." I pointed. "There's Henry James. There's Hemingway." And as I drew his attention to these authors whom he'd surely read and surely, for the most part, revered, each face on the wall seemed to flinch from John's lumbering gaze.

"I don't like that one peering there," he said, frowning at George Bernard Shaw. His hands crept up around his head, where they encountered his beret. He registered a look of horror and pulled it off, scowling at the woolen lump now belly-up on the table, as if some propriety had been breached. He seemed continually to appall himself—*this* slip of etiquette; *that* act of fumbling senescence. And then he looked up with his inimitable twinkle and said, "Margaret wanted to get me a placard for my car, in case I fall into a temporary illness."

I waited for the explanation, or at the very least the trigger, for his recollection. It didn't come. He thought the punch line had already been delivered.

"Placard," I prompted. He blinked, forcing himself to cast back over the last moment for what had seized his mirth. "I realized," he began, leaning forward, his fingertips worrying the empty sugar packet, "that it isn't temporary at all. I realized that this will not go away."

He leaned back. A "nothing to be done" set of jaw hardened his features, although the little sparkle in his eyes remained. "*This* is no temporary illness," he repeated.

And then, with the sort of exquisitely bad timing that reflected my miserable failure not to flinch, I blurted, "This will be our last day together." I hemmed. I hawed. I released the trotting ponies of excuses, which faltered on guilt and the shame for failing him. In the end, my vow not to flinch had proven lame.

"Ah, you're leaving me," he said.

I opened my mouth to release more lies: "Maybe we could go to the symphony some afternoon, or movies—we both love movies—or sometimes we could go have tea with Margaret." It was easier to believe the sweet prevarications than to look directly into his sad, adoring eyes and, without flinching, say, "Good-bye. This is just too hard."

IT WAS FLATTERING TO THINK I MIGHT SUSTAIN A RELA-tionship with John, even were I to quit my job companioning for the Lutherans. Others with less convoluted minds than mine might easily initiate amusements to lend variety to an old man's days. But I had proven to be a flincher, after all. I could offer going to symphony, for example; I could envision us attending with delight, but then, our time up, I'd leave and start my car, only to feel mystified by an encroaching and unwavering dread. Surely, healthy, cheerful others would not be paralyzed by dread but would get on with it, the modest task of making an old man happy. But I couldn't.

I had been warning Harriet, and Margaret and Kate, his daughters, that John was an accident waiting to happen—pardon the cliché—and my warnings had gone unheeded. It was as if the will it took to wedge entrenched behavior from its trough tipped all into a parallel and wrenching immobility. I understood this. The will it took to eke an intelligent, sustained response from Mother or an impish, fond grin from the Father would sometimes launch me toward the bottle or a nap. I wanted some power to impact John's perilous situation, credence given to my observations. It was all no good—the neglected floor-length curtains, showering dust when brushed against; the ancient kilim, rotting where John had watered; the treacherous, steep stairway, suggesting Tosca and the parapet; Leonardo singing for his supper, and God only knew when he'd had it last; the narrow pantry clotted with cardboard cases of French Colombard. It was all a slippery slope, building toward disaster. And we all knew it, *but* . . .

I wanted my perceptions and affection to influence some happy outcome—the sale of the enormous, cluttered home; a move to a stimulating retirement community.

A few weeks after I stopped working with John, I learned that he had fallen on the floor in his kitchen and lain there, in and out of consciousness, for three days. I don't remember who found him or if he managed to rescue himself. I had developed a cordial telephone relationship with Margaret, his eldest, and it was she who shared the news.

"We'll be moving him out of rehab, when he can walk again, and into assisted living. Finally!" Margaret said.

"Finally," I echoed. "So, even though it was horrible, his accident, some good came of it."

She averred. I commiserated. But commiseration wasn't parity. I did not know my place.

I had felt something toward this man that I had not felt, for a long time anyway, with the Father—a flow of affection, a twinkle, uncomplicated care, respect, colloquy, banter. I wanted to insinuate myself into the peculiar circle—John and Margaret and Kate. I longed to mean more to John and his daughters than might ever a $7.29-per-hour, unskilled employee. Our conversations, Margaret's and mine, *were* meaningful. We understood each other as "university brats" with strong-willed, charismatic, rigid fathers.

Here, I believed, was a scenario so much more engaging than mine; mine was a solo performance playing to an empty house. John had let me in; Margaret, in our half a dozen conversations, had shown respect for my observations. This had triggered my atavistic yearning to belong, a vulnerability that could strip me of good judgment.

It made me think about the dog.

SHE CAME TO US, OUR SMALL FAMILY, FAR TOO YOUNG. Five weeks, in fact—weaned but unsocialized. Taken from the litter prematurely, she hadn't had time for her nature to emerge in relation to her siblings. Now, originally, I was not for this dog, was adamantly a *not*-dog person. Give me a cat any day. Plus, being a mere five weeks old, she looked like a fetus—a wiggly, pale, stubby, fetal *thing*—and oh! I was revolted and wanted nothing to do with it.

One night, over family dinner, the idea of a puppy, jokingly, had been floated as a surrogate for Susannah, whose sister, Lily, would soon be college-bound. Dana, my wife, missed the innuendo—*joke*—and before any thoughtfulness could be brought to the proposition, Susannah, well everyone, really, except me, was caught in an updraft of giddy excitement. Before the salad course, they'd already earmarked half a dozen breeds.

As the puppy grew, she developed problems. We called the trainer. He assessed and explained. The problematic behavior, as I recall, had to do with the puppy's teeth and the objects they encountered—hands, chair legs, walls (yes, she ate the plaster off the pantry walls), pant legs, hands, most especially hands. She had become a terror. Her name was Bee.

"Understand," said Jeff the trainer, "if Bee had been allowed to find her rank in the pack, probably she'd be a very sweet dog. I can see it's her nature to be submissive."

We expressed surprise.

"But since she doesn't know her place, she's trying to be in charge. She's doing this because she's anxious. You're her pack, and she's anxious and confused."

I said something about how that made two of us.

"Three," Dana added.

"Four," Susannah echoed.

"Now, what we won't know," Jeff continued, "is whether it's too late."

That sounded serious. "I don't understand," I said. "She's just a puppy."

"We'll try to teach her her place and then see if that makes her less anxious," and, so saying, he flipped her onto her back and held her down.

It was impressive. He hooked his hand through her collar

to protect himself from the slashing jaws and pinned her chest. She protested horribly—screaming, teeth chattering, kicking. The three of us wrung our hands and clutched our breasts.

"Drama queen," I snorted.

"Actually, yes," said Jeff. "This isn't hurting her a bit. It's pissing her off. It's surprising her. But watch. In about two seconds, she'll go completely limp."

In two seconds, she went completely limp, and he praised and petted her, and she smiled and licked his hand.

"You'll have to dominate her every time she gets mouthy," he said.

This seemed fun to me—to bully the fetus for her own good. To put her in her place.

It went on for months. When walking, Bee got it into her mind to take the leash between her teeth and leap and pull like a fish on a line. Or she'd decide that she'd had enough walking and would sit squarely, solidly, mulishly in the middle of the street. Or nibble on the hand that held the leash. Dana would often return from their walks bloody.

It came to pass that I would love the dog. This end result, or ongoing process, was due to the power of relationship and was hard won. I am grateful to the dog. She brought disruption, inconvenience, and raw need into the home, and the opportunity to experience—with time, a little money, and effort—the satisfaction of growth and transformation. Curiosity played the largest role. In its absence, resentment and rage had come to prevail. Curiosity opened my mind to the possibility that this process was more interesting than merely a battle of wills. The dog didn't know her place. That was interesting.

There is nothing linear about growth—the shift away

from destructive behaviors, toward change and understanding. The musical chairs of mind neither honor nor acknowledge the conventional apprehension of time but occupy a simultaneity, and I think about Bee and her crisis of place and what healed it. John's place had been the university, as was my father's. John lost his place because of university politics, the shrinking classics department, and a retirement that did not honor him with an office. John was out of place in the cavernous home, and his latest mishap proved it. Now he was in a bed somewhere in a nursing home.

I could not accept my place in appropriate relationship to any of my old charges, but especially not to John. My role, my place, was too painfully limited, and wanting more was sad, perilous, even. Nor could I effect a change in John's situation. It had proven impossible to go on.

⇌

Commentary:

MY FATHER'S DEATH

MY FATHER DIED IN DECEMBER 2012, THREE WEEKS SHY of turning ninety-eight. He had been, in his way, a great and honored man. His life was shaped by a long and distinguished career. At nearly ninety-eight, he deemed himself finally, *fully* retired, having, two years prior to that, risen at eight each morning to make his way up "the mountain" (a slight, woodsy rise above Lehigh University) to his lab, where he met his colleague of fifty-some years. There, two impassioned engineers in their final years worked to formulate rust-resistant steel, an "invention" with significant ramifications for the durability and longevity of infrastructure everywhere.

For so many years, my father had cultivated a Self: professor; head of the metallurgy department; dean of the graduate school; consultant; president of this and that; king of steel; doting husband; dutiful father; lover of cats and all things Pennsylvania Dutch. How long could he get away with it, maintaining a distinguished, witty, courtly, intact self? Ninety-seven years—almost ninety-eight! Would his luck continue, and there emerge a beautiful preparedness for dying?

His increasing physical frailty (he had begun to curl in upon himself, like a fallen leaf) was its own process, it seemed, separate from the mind's. My father had not prepared to leave that dwelling place, to imagine a state beyond the self his mind had crafted. He did not, in the end, have a "good death," a peaceful transition, did not depart with the elegance with which he had lived.

I HAVE CONFESSED THAT ONE OF THE JUSTIFICATIONS for taking minimum-wage employment with "my" old people was that they stood as proxy for my aging parents.

The three thousand miles between us functioned as a boundary, assuring we'd see each other no more than we deemed necessary to maintain the civil bond. Nevertheless, guilt was a price that subsidized that journey. John had functioned as my father proxy. My deep appreciation of the man, especially of his maddening eccentricities, enabled me to throw some fondness, like a scrim, over the impressions historically held of my father.

Our relationship was contentious. Over the years, I experienced our differences as a personal torment, finding it wise to steer clear of personal disclosure, maintaining enough civility to assure my yearly Christmas check. From across the country I'd make my weekly phone calls, and as he began his decline, I was tossed by conflicting emotions—the horror of it; resentment to find myself suddenly a major player; boredom; guilt; occasional flecks of compassion; guilt that I could not muster more. After all, it was one thing to picture the father as a curled leaf, another to open to his suffering. With his decline, what began as duty—fraught, ambivalent—stirred and shifted. Duty enabled compassion.

DANA AND I FLEW BACK TO BETHLEHEMPENNSYLVANIA four times in the late fall–winter of 2012, covering every major holiday. Name one, we were either in the air or on a highway —Thanksgiving, Christmas, New Year's, Martin Luther King Day. My father's timing was consistent, I'll give him that, though not convenient. The first trip back, on Thanksgiving, having "enjoyed" a dinner of leftover chicken and Brussels sprouts in a tinny rental car, we arrived at night. He'd been discharged from the hospital after a sickening accident—late one night, he fell over backward and broke his neck. Home would now be not his spacious, monumentally furnished apartment but the second floor of the skilled-nursing facility at the Moravian Village, his retirement community.

We arrived and walked through the corridor separating the two wings—the healthy residents from those shuttled into skilled nursing. Up the elevator to the second floor; check in at the nurses' station; "yes, it is all right to visit this late." We were shown his door. There, a stunning view of the tiny, flailing father clinging with skeletal hand to the arm of his wheelchair, a stricken look on his face, hanging like a baby bird caught by a talon. His neck brace held his head aloft. I found myself quickly in front of the nurses' station, crying, "Help! Father falling." The nurses rallied, rushed, wrestled him into his chair. That was a Moment. There would follow many more.

Our next trip would be made soon after that, in the following week, in fact. He was hospitalized again, this time for a breathing crisis. While there and barely conscious (his living will firmly directed, "No extreme measures"), he received an order for exploratory surgery from his "good friend" and cardiologist, Dr. T. This was done. My father now had not only a broken neck but an eight-inch incision in his abdomen. There in the bed, in the terrible gown, lay the flattened, brittle shape of him—GN tube up his nose, oxygen looped around his neck, restraints on his hands like mittens. Had it not been for them, he'd be thrashing, pulling at the hateful tubes and stitches.

By now, the swiftness of his slide further intensified and quickened. He could no longer speak; a mix of weakness, intubation, and a failing esophageal sphincter diminished that ability. His Self had peeled away like bark to reveal a simple set of needs and raw emotion. The emotions ranged from brief happiness to terror, a range without the mediating role of his intellect, Victorian sensibilities, and judgment. This was our new agenda—to be with him wholly and utterly: to be with, to breathe with, to love this old man, my father, and open to the incremental losses with their stunning curriculum in impermanence.

⇌

WHAT IS IT THAT DETERMINES WHO IS WILLING TO OPEN, who not? My father, in his way, had turned a corner. At ninety-two, resigned to solitude and a view aimed backward, he found love. Able to drop his identification as a widower, he opened his heart. Her name was Grace. She was a younger woman—ninety to his then ninety-two. In one phone conversation, he disclosed, "I have met someone. We've been companions for some time." He hastened to add, "It is platonic."

The openness was unusual for my father, not a man given to self-reflection or, in my experience, to sharing his feelings or demonstrating a particular interest in privileging them over science. This news of Grace surprised and gladdened me. I don't know what opened my father to love, but it was clear when I saw them together that a tenderness, a regard, and a thread of silliness ran between them. Other residents and friends—lookers-on to their late love—diminished it, in my mind, by calling them "the lovebirds," finding their affection cute, the way first love and all its fumbling eagerness is regarded, a diminution of something more profound. After all, what courage it must take to say yes to love, knowing that each day brings you closer to losing it, leaving love to exhausted loneliness once again.

His opening touched me. But had my father found the courage to say yes to that, making the inevitability of loss that much more poignant, or did it signify the delusion that he was going, in his mind, to live forever? I chose to believe the former and so began to salvage fondness out of the wreck that had been our "love," and took his opening as an invitation. I, too, opened.

Openness repaid us with many moments:

My father, sunk and shriveled in the hospital bed, flanked.

Dana and I on one side of his bed; Dr. T. and his wife, J., adamantly beside him, on the other. Albeit reserved, we were doing battle. Dr. T., my age exactly, sandy-haired, with the aura of a good and righteous boy, albeit arrogant, had, in my absence, passed himself off as the medical power of attorney and, being a doctor, had never been challenged by the hospital staff. This man with his confused agenda wanted to persuade my father to accept a surgically implanted feeding tube. This ran against the wishes expressed in the living will, which Dr. T. had in his possession. Dr. T. and J. on one side, Dana and I on the other, we "argued" back and forth across the battlefield of his body. ("Pop, do you understand what a tube will mean?" "Robert, *remember*, we discussed the procedure this morning. You could go back home and live!")

The hospital social worker, drawn into the drama as much by the ethical breach as by the poignancy, and Dr. B., the hospice physician—lean, Chekhovian, kind—bore witness to the charade of compassion unfolding over my father's head. From time to time Dr. B. interjected, calmly stating what such a procedure would mean, restraining his own bafflement and anger.

Finally my father sputtered, gasped: "not civilized; do not want . . ." emerged. All of us straightened, leaned in to hear the fragile, wispy phrases. Dr. B. asked him to repeat. My father, who had not spoken a clear word, let alone a sentence, for weeks, managed, "It is not dignified. I do not want the tube." He smiled, sensing triumph, looked at Dr. T., his "good friend," and whispered, "I'm sorry."

Dr. T., deflated, stepped back, lowered his head in defeat and resignation; J. scraped together scarf, gloves, and papers, intractable smile remaining on her face.

I wanted to applaud and weep—the stupendous effort; his words that indicated his understanding that he had freed himself to die. It was done; it was decided.

"Robert, do you know what this means?" Dr. T. tried one last time to tyrannize. "Starvation! You will die."

My father nodded sweetly. His restraints removed, he looked almost naked, tiny, in his patterned gown. He was eager to go home. Home would be the second-floor skilled-nursing unit for however long, and what that implied. Home, in this regard, took on a secondary meaning of release.

And this: a rapid discharge followed his heroic declaration. In his old bed, still in the "gown," he was yet to be trousered and wrapped in the old brown sweater. As we entered his room, we heard Grace's scooter behind us. We waved her ahead, wanting them to have their moment. In she whirred, and my father, perhaps hearing the familiar sound of her scooter or something more, looked up from his pillows and beamed—the purest, unobscured beam of affection—as Grace approached the bed. There they remained for an extended moment of love commingling with sorrow.

He had indeed come "home." An ordeal had been suffered, and survived, but yes had been said to allowing the natural process. Grace did not yet know the implication, and so the moment contained the joy and relief that followed their absence from each other, and perhaps the hope that their forward-looking time together could resume.

AND YET I FOUND MYSELF WANTING TO SHRIEK, YOU *are not doing this at all well, this dying!* You *are utterly undoing each and every lifetime achievement award, every accolade, every crisp bit of ego chip that has accrued to the monument that was your life.* You *are blowing all that in a few terrible weeks of unseemly decline, and pulling us along with you!*

However, there is a paradox that comes with the kind of tending we, Dana and I, determined to do. Allowing this process—its intense awfulness—leads to heightened senses, which lead in turn (at least in retrospect) to an increased sense of being alert and alive.

I FIND MYSELF REPEATING THIS OFTEN: "MY FATHER FELL backward and broke his neck," as if trying to make myself believe that this really happened. I find myself wanting still to blame him for this terrible fall, to admonish, "How many times did I tell you, Pop, always to use your walker?" To blame. As if, underneath this, I am hanging onto the belief that there is always some choice, some control within our reach, and not the chilling facts of disintegration, annihilation, the self mysteriously dissolved.

SIXTEEN

⇌

The Perfidy of Things

I HAD BEEN INVITED BACK TO BETHLEHEMPENN-
sylvania with the looming threat to celebrate another birthday
—*this might be Your Mother's Last* [you are invited to fill in any
festive last occasion]. Since each of us preferred the idea of
each other to the thorny fact, the occupation of a saccharine
past was the only turf we could agree on. Long-ago memories,
of when I toddled forth in pinafores and Mary Janes or was
swung like a squealing whirligig in the arms of the Father, had
become overly remembered and chronically reviewed. And so,
you will ask, how did we celebrate my birthday now, on this
latest trip? Did the Stouts, this time around, carouse, noise-
makers twirled in eager hands, conehead hats set at a rakish
angle, cake and candles marched toward the groaning board?
Crab cakes were ordered and procured from my parents'
favorite restaurant. I noticed that the Bach CD I'd bought for
Mother had been deposited at my place at the table.

"What's this?" I asked. "Didn't you like it?"

"What would I do with it?" she asked flatly.

"It was a gift," I said back flatly. "For *your* birthday."

"What do you want for *your* birthday?" she asked, as if picking up her cue.

"I don't know, " I said. "What do you have in mind?"

Did I expect a present? I expected—rather, hoped—that some portion of the day would be free of disappointment. So far, I was waiting still.

Mother looked at Father, and steadily, he looked back at her. She said, with little affect but with a feverish look of inspiration in her eyes, "I was thinking you might like the Fur."

This alarmed me.

Hers was no ordinary, clichéd fur. Hers was a knockout, the Monica Vitti of furs. It seemed to have a pedigree: "blush-dyed, black cross mink," platinum blond laced with silver, the two subtly contrasting tones teased into relationship by thin strands of black. It was full length, which, in Mother's case, shrinking as she was, meant floor length now. Generously cuffed, it was cut in a classic style.

I had been introduced to Mother's mink soon after she bought it. She adored her fur, as if its acquisition signified the arrival at a station in life characterized by dignity and respect. The coat conferred something upon her, even though elegance did not attach to Mother by virtue of the coat. Huddled and round inside it, she looked like a honey bear. It was beautiful, but wrong in many ways, a response I did not share with my parents when I met the coat, because they were, after all, my *parents*, the big people—those who knew what they wanted and had a right to want what they wanted as well, and to consume accordingly. But in this time of mink, I'd begun to notice certain disquieting behaviors. The parents who had instilled in me a latticework of right and wrong, values of frugality and consumer conservatism, had, as they crept toward their high seventies, begun to spend their money in insurgent ways—a kitchen remodel coinciding with my mother's lost interest in the culinary arts; a vacuum cleaner whose amazing features were spoken of in the hushed tones reserved for religious experiences and that cost $1,000; a Cadillac. Were these sprees a prelude to dementia?

Because objects were, in our family, love's proxy, I'd made those six trips back and forth in the year before my mother's death, allegedly to get familiar with her estate. The sheer quantity of Mother's things enrobed my mind like LSD—the contents of her drawers, trunks, and room-length closets; her abandoned coin collection; twenty Krugerrands; silver presidential plates issued by the Franklin Mint, a complete set of ugly heads engraved in silver; jewelry, pieces of and of no value; and, of course, the fur. A delusion of affluence would begin to cloud my thinking, but the raw truth was my yearning. Tricked by fiction's deathbed scenes, I yearned for the love between two people equally committed to finding a language for their complicated relationship, even though it was the very passion of the one and the coolness of the other that in some ways defined the complication. Such love would not suddenly manifest. How could it?

And, with inauspicious clarity, I recalled the mink's role in one Family Christmas Moment. It was the winter of '99. For years, Mother's greatest wish had been to travel as a family unit to her Favorite Place in Life, Tide's Inn. This was a family-owned hotel-resort located in Irvington, Virginia, in the old plantation country along the backwaters of the Chesapeake Bay. Every year for years, starting in October, she'd beg me to come with them. After years of this, she wore me down. Even then, her collection of maladies had reduced her to eighty-some pounds, a dreadful and toxic cycle of antibiotic medications; an atrophied musculature; a paralyzing terror, triggered by her osteoporosis, of ever going outside; and a touch of dementia. What was a little existential dread and holiday-travel phobia compared with my mother's need to have bolstered her last-ditch attempt to make a Perfect Happy Family Moment?

For Mother the main highlight, besides getting to make an appearance at her Favorite Place in Life as a Perfect Family, was that she could wear the Fur. Furs, any and all, at Tide's Inn seemed a prerequisite to participating in the holiday festivities, where everyone was over seventy and all the females were displaying their furs.

The day before the day of Christmas Eve, the minute we got there, it started snowing. This was a pretty thing at first, adding atmosphere and gaiety, allowing the guests that self-congratulatory moment experienced by the well fed and the swaddled, able to witness from deep chairs the weather turning foul. All night it snowed. By morning, ice was falling from the sky, hissing and covering the snow and sealing it with a thick glaze. Branches, power lines, berries, steps, stairs, leaves, railings, all things man-made and all things natural, had become enchanted and entrapped by ice. And then it snowed again. Able to bear no more, trees broke apart. In the furious aftermath, to walk outside was to court concussion, deafness, gashes, and nasty falls. Huge tree limbs littered the grounds. The air resounded with the crack of exploding trees. It was malignant Stravinsky, relentless Charles Ives, pure dissonance, percussion whose point it is to flay alive.

Inside, the old people huddled, females in their furs, males in blankets, curled over littered copies of the *Wall Street Journal* and the *New York Times*. The innkeepers, four cheerful brothers, kept us steadily updated. By Christmas Eve, the power lines had fallen and the entire county was freezing and dark. There was no heat inside the inn. And with power gone, there would be no famous Christmas dinner, which Mother had been looking forward to, well, for years. Most especially mourned in the defeat of her expectations would be the cascading mountain of desserts. And with power gone, there would be no light with which to see not only Christmas dinner and dessert but competing furs and jewelry. Disappointment tangled with fear, because with power gone there would also be no heat, no light, no running water—no bathing, no brushing, and, perhaps most horrible of all, no flushing.

It was beginning to feel like the *Titanic*.

Upon every step of the wide spiral staircase, candles appeared. Also in the narrow upstairs hallway, candles were placed every few feet beside the wall. Remember, the majority of the guests were people who no longer saw as well as they used to, people who walked with aids, people who wore long, trailing fur coats over long, trailing gowns. Did I mention the long drapes that glorified the curving staircase wall; that the candles burned only inches from the drapes; that old people crept unsupervised up and down the stairs in their long coats, with their reduced vision and compromised balance? I have never been so resigned to death in all my life.

And then, to palliate the discontent, and with an eye to the profits of next season, the brothers announced an open bar —free drinks for all, morning, noon, and night. Where were the adults in charge? I saw no evidence that this had been identified as folly; I felt compelled to pray over the twin horrors of the candles *and* the open bar.

On the night before Christmas, it was not true that creatures were not stirring. I swear I heard rats in the larder, mice giggling in the walls. I imagined the sputter and catch of flame, the insatiable roar of heavy cloth caught on fire, the eleventh-hour merriment of those swilling nonstop in the bar —old wayfarers clinging via scotch or bourbon to each other in the worsening ordeal. I heard the groan of the by-now-frozen pipes as yet another guest, on the sly, tried flushing.

Two emergency generators kept the kitchen more or less running so that the food on hand, which needed no preparation, could be assembled. Into the dining room we filed, lumpy, dark figures—many, like Mother, bundled in their furs —to consume these rations in compulsory candlelight. We shuffled to our tables, dejected and embarrassed. Beauty, after all, required witness, and the competing finery would go unseen. In the shadows cast by candles we looked like bears, looming with massive, hairy arms over paper plates.

You couldn't look out the tall windows onto the endless ice and not raise a hand to keep your beating heart from being iced over. Collectively, we shuddered. Soon the ice would penetrate the dining room and encase us in its frigid sheen. We would all die there, plastic flatware poised between frozen lips and table, glasses half raised to mouths rigidly agape, frozen eyeballs staring. We were all becoming ice.

But even amid all this gustatory disappointment—the glistening hunks of beef, unroasted; the Christmas fowl, unbaked—Mother still anticipated her meals with an innocent belief that all would be made better, that the good fairy was afoot, or a-wing, ready to sweep a wand over the icy disaster, and, presto! Lights, aromas, the sounds of happy diners, the holiday meal restored. What dreams lay in the tiers of ornate desserts and the choices of fowl or fish or beef, the faux sophistication of the menu I can only guess at. Like a child, my mother wanted the sweetness of her imagined pleasures to appear and multiply like puffy clouds and, unlike clouds, to endure.

My last task before heading to the bar was to get my parents to their room without catching them on fire—up the spiral staircase and past the incipient conflagration of the candle flames, down the dark hallway, into the sepulchral chill of their room, into their separate beds and under covers.

"Bed," Mother croaked, as we shuffled through the shadows in the hallway.

Their room was barely warmer than the air outside the windows. "Don't you want to brush your teeth first?" I asked.

"No," she said with the adamancy of a ten-year-old. "I won't."

"Mummie, you'll feel better if you brush your teeth," I said, appealing to that part of her that knew better.

"Put me to bed now," she said. "Tuck me in."

Unsure how to negotiate our role-reversal moment, I pressed: "How about putting on your nightie?"

"I am not going to put on my nightie. I am not going to take off my clothes."

Ever the engineer, the Father puttered nonchalantly with the contents of his pockets, scattering coins and such over the frigid bureau top. Briskly he unbuttoned, and shuffled to the dark bathroom with his pajamas draped over his arm. The Father derived deep comfort from the observance of routines. Despair would not overcome his tooth brushing.

Horrified by the image of Mother falling into bed in her formal wear and topcoat, with dirty teeth to boot, I turned the covers down and addressed her firmly. "Mummie, let me help you get undressed." But my mother, resolute, aimed her body at the bed. She dropped and laid on her back like a corpse in the big, blond mink. "I will sleep in my coat," she told the ceiling.

Mother's revolt only added to the anarchistic holiday, where bears hunched at tables over tiny dinner plates, and nights fell fast, bringing terrible things with them out of the sky, and any minute we could perish—a possibility heightened by inebriated elders—and unflushable wastes accumulated in 187 toilet bowls. Clearly the things of the world had tumbled out of order; God had fled his heaven and was sitting downstairs at the open bar.

On Christmas morning, they closed the inn. Another storm was brewing, and we were sent away. The sun blazed for a moment, glancing off the ice with a brilliance that pierced the brain. As we stood waiting for the car, Mother turned and asked, "Would you like to wear my coat? Put it on, and we'll take a picture."

"Robert," she called to my father, who was standing right beside her. "Do take a picture." I thought of all the famous women photographed for those classy fur-coat ads—Lillian Hellman most especially, because she was a writer, too. She was a homely woman, but in that moment—floor-length, dark, and sexy—she looked redeemed. Chin upthrust, insinuating leg, she was proof of the transforming power of mink.

My black wool coat hung on my mother's shoulders. She was smiling. Valets and bellhops gamely offered us a wide berth as the Father jostled the camera. I wished, then, in the fur, that our momentary exchange of coats could have brought a corresponding exchange of information, that it would enter through my pores and transmit these details of Mother's life that had collectively rushed us all *here*, to this place, in the glaring disappointment of this day.

Much later, I received two snapshots in the mail, both slightly out of focus—no surprise. The Father put little stock in the recording of Family Moments, acquiescing out of an obligation to humor my mother's female whims, as he must have thought them. In the first, I'd not yet struck my pose and was caught struggling with the big blond pelt, shrugging it over my shoulders, eyes cast down upon the icy, limb-strewn ground. In the second, I'd struck my pose, my Lillian Hellman pose, but the top of my head was not with or on me. I was an upturned plane of face. A thin, dark line marked where hair began. A jagged line of crimson from the sumac shrub behind inserted itself into the frame like blood from a laceration. The coat, of course, looked splendid—the gifted sibling who excels whatever the activity or art—making fake food out of papier-mâché, mastering a Bach partita, or simply securing the affections, with little effort and seeming joy, of her parents. The mink shone; I was its ugly sister.

The mink was bad news all around with its grim associations. There in my mind would lay my mother under the big, blond fur, the corpse of Christmas Eve. There in the snapshot I would stand forever enrobed and headless in the brittle world of ice, while old people, stunned and all around me, fled disaster.

⇌

THAT WAS THE GIFT THAT MOTHER HAD THREATENED TO give me over our crab cake birthday dinner. Under a cotton blanket festooned with yellow daisies back in Bethlehem-pennsylvania, her breath rippled up and down her sunken chest. She rubbed her feet together the way babies do, a kind of greeting among toes. She was reviewing documents that had no meaning—a plane ticket and subsequent itinerary from 1970; carbon copies of the home care service; photos I had sent her two years earlier from my trip to Utah, which she told me to take back.

I said, "They're yours. You *asked* me for those pictures."

"What will I do with them?" she asked flatly.

"They were a gift," I said, as with the Bach, flatly back.

Her heart bobbed wildly beneath her bones, a balloon pummeled by stormy weather. Her little bird hands joined, quivering, around a mug of tepid Sanka. We were almost to good-bye. I pulled a chair beside her bed and held her hand. She called out, "Robert."

Teetering and devoted, he rose from the sofa. She wanted us three to make a circle. He hesitated and then lowered himself onto the tiny wooden chair behind me, so that I was looking at Mother and he was looking at me looking at Mother. Why, I wondered, would it not occur to him to connect our dots; place himself *in* space—a good and helpful preposition—*across* from me; *beside* me; *with* us—somewhere in space that created an arrangement in which torqueing and straining were not paramount?

I looked at these parents, locking eyes above my head and beaming at each other. This was a Really Bad Seating Moment. My neck cramped, trying to see him behind and her in front, at an angle, to insert myself into their geometry and be seen.

And then I understood something: they were locked; they were inseparable; they would always float above me in this way. Theirs was a contract. Theirs was a code—Mother's million inane questions; Father's million definitive replies—as they held me in their peripheral vision and conducted endless dialogues about the size and shape of things. They were like little salt and pepper shakers.

What had been their contract? The mystery of it nagged me, always had.

If only we could have said it to each other, could have arranged our chairs so we could look, without contortions, at each other, could together have named and grieved the losses. Love among us would remain a sedimentary thing—pressured by guilt and envy and a sly disinterest nurtured by the absence of egg and sperm, the lack of the pregnancy drama, the glue of biology's twists and turns.

⇌

Commentary:

Naked Underneath the Fur

AND SO THE FUR WAS *MINE*, A WORD INFUSED WITH HOPE of happy gain. I had fallen under its charm when it was *not mine* and, with some success, had risen above a demented craving for the thing, withdrawing into my mental shrine room whenever it was mentioned by Mother or her household help or friends. It was beautiful, and it was *mine*. However, to wear any kind of fur in the conservation-minded, nature-loving Pacific Northwest, where I would be doomed to bring it, would have been to court disdain. Animal-rights people, who are scary and do not wait patiently for explanations extolling the mother-daughter bond, could be felt to hover in large numbers, waiting to hurl eggs and spray blood. Adding to my reluctance to be signaled out was the determining fact of climate—it's not cold enough to wear fur here. To dispel all temptation to wear the thing, I researched mink and learned that four might share a cage whose dimensions equal one foot by three. In their natural habitat, the animals spend 60 percent to 70 percent of their happy lives in the water, in *solitary* pleasure. As is the case with any blended family living in tight quarters, on the farm the minks take bites out of one another. Confinement creates contagious diseases. Think Lower East Side Manhattan in the latter half of the nineteenth century. Fleas, lice, ticks, mites contribute to collective merriment.

On one of the commercial websites, there was actually an argument using ecology as a justification for raising fur. The farms were said to *help* restore the land to balance, but the claims defied credulity. The diet fed the caged animals, according to the site, "spared" landfills literally tons of nasty, rotting by-products from the meat, poultry, egg, dairy, and fish industries. To claim that this is good for the minks and the environment simply does not jibe. Picture just one item on the mink menu, and it will set your gag reflex in motion. This distortion, that the farms are doing their bit by recycling *and* in the process nourishing the animals, makes Marie Antoinette's "let them eat cake" seem almost a kindness.

And so I traded one greed for another and determined to sell the thing and make a bundle. When she bought it many years ago, Mother paid $10,000, and that was on sale! Imagine what it must be worth now! My anticipated profit would function as a paycheck for all these stupid Bethlehempennsylvania efforts. My pulse raced; I was convinced of the coat's value, unimpeded by the capriciousness of style and depreciation. With mounting joy, I fanaticized about my fortune and called consignment stores. I called with Mother's original sales receipt before me and practiced saying "blush-dyed, black cross mink" so that I would not stumble over my words, so that clerks would think I knew my stuff.

Repeatedly, I was met with a silence of the "so what?" kind. That might have been followed with "we don't carry furs" or "we stopped carrying furs" or the merely malignant "ha ha." Euphoria transmogrified to panic.

"Well, dear, for example, we sold a very lovely full-length fur last week," I was told. "It had originally been bought for six thousand dollars."

"Yes, yes?" I would beg the voice to continue.

"We let it go for two hundred," the voice replied.

I couldn't even calculate the plummeting percentage. My fortune had taken a beating. Now, you'd think it wouldn't really matter, because when I did not own the fur, did I expect $10,000 to visit me out of nowhere? Greed said yes, but I should have slipped gracefully back to my impecunious homeostasis, totally at home in the worries—existential and actual—engendered by attempts at self-support. Selling Mother's mink would, I had assumed, offer a little antidote, a little comfort, like being bungeed out of penury toward relief.

I am the sort of person who has never once managed to sell one item through the newspaper. There is a karmic explanation: I do not read newspapers. But I had grown desperate about the mink, and so I wrote an ad.

"Classy," it said. "Classic." (Who could refuse?) "Yours for only $6,500." The meek print "obo" followed. I tucked the mink back in its royal-blue satin casing and prepared to wait. It was the week of Thanksgiving. I readied myself to give thanks.

MY FIRST CALL WAS FROM A HUSBAND OF A WIFE WHO also had a mink coat that she wanted to sell, and could I advise her? I do not remember my reply as kind. The second call was from a man named Christopher. He would be in town for the Thanksgiving holiday, he said, visiting friends and family. He was a very nice man, if talkative, and soon it became clear to me that if I was going to keep running the ad, I'd better raise the price to reflect what it cost me to do phone therapy with my prospective buyers. Christopher's questions about the coat led me to suspect he was not asking on behalf of a wife or a sister. They indicated self-interest. Finally, I asked him his line of work.

"I have a high-end consignment shop in Vegas," he replied, after a moment's hesitation. "Actually," he added, "I'm retired."

"From what?" I asked.

"I was a female impersonator."

I began to learn more about Christopher than he wished, it was apparent, to learn about the fur. I learned that he grew up in Seattle and on rainy days played dress-up with his sister. I learned that, as far as Christopher was concerned, he got the looks in the family. His sister, he said, was a dog. I learned Mummy had dressed him up as a fairy princess one Halloween, and each successive Halloween, his costumes had edged a little closer toward a bona fide gender blur. Fairy princess led to prom queen, which in turn inspired whole portfolios of les femmes fatales. One day in adolescence, Christopher rummaged around in his mother's closet. She was an airline stewardess away on a trip. He found—in his words—"a beautiful powder-blue Delta Airlines uniform" (it was at this stage in our conversation that I began to doubt Christopher's "high-end" taste). He put in on and realized, *I could pass!* A star was born.

Finally, I cut in. He had taken up half the morning, and I hadn't bagged a sale. He assured me that he was serious about the mink. We left it at he'd call around Thanksgiving.

I hung up, excited. The gap between tiny, status-driven Mother in her coat and a drag queen, after all, was just ironic self-regard.

A week later, there was a message on my machine. He'd bought other things for the store, he said. He was sorry, he said. He wished me the best of luck.

A week after that, there was a message on my machine from a Mike So-and-So, who worked at a Chevrolet dealership in Bellevue. A car salesman did not offer nearly the poetic justice that a female impersonator in Mother's coat did. Nevertheless, a sale was a sale. I returned his call and was put on hold for ten minutes, because he was with a customer. This repeated itself three times. Fifteen minutes later, still on hold, I felt my fortune slip away, and the small hope that, at least, the ad would pay for itself. I severed the connection.

It moved from its sheath onto a Shaker hook in the hallway. To offset pomp, I hung a worn baseball cap on top. Friends, upon seeing it, would wonder. I'd explain, slip it on, and invite admiration. I disclosed the original price, how little it was worth at present. They'd exclaim, "You can*not* sell it. It was your mother's, and she loved it." Reluctantly, I have come to agree.

Every winter, there arrives at least one cold snap in Seattle. The temperature hovers between the single digits and the teens; the sky, after the turbulent, torrential rains of November, undergoes an extraordinary change, and its blue is clear and cutting. Sometimes snow, ice, and wind paralyze the city, and when that's true, Dana and I take the fur off her hook, spread it on the bed, and huddle. It adds weight, a tactile opulence, and atavistic comfort.

Or I take pleasure in picturing myself wearing it outside and I am naked underneath it. The time would have to be dusk or early dawn, so that my strutting would not alarm the neighbors or set off the mink activists surely passing by. I would stick furtively to the shadows of the hedge, twigs between my toes, hedge bits in my hair, surprisingly snug in the envelope of Mother, in truth honoring her in my own, odd way.

SEVENTEEN

⇌

Love and Final Trips Remembered

AS MY PROSPECTS OF SELLING THE MINK DWINDLED AND greed gave way to resignation, I began again to worry, *Should I get a job?* It wasn't a worry driven strictly by financial woe. It had more to do with feeling crazy. In those years preceding the lure of family life, I felt quite isolated. Between my trips to Bethlehempennsylvania and the minutia-studded time spent there, I wondered, where brewed social life; where gathered like-minded companions; where dwelt rapport and joie de vivre?

When in Bethlehempennsylvania, I had ascribed best-friend status to my journal. Never without notebook open on my lap, pen speeding across receptive pages, I continuously observed, recorded, chortled, and connected myself, feverishly, to meaning.

I engaged with the Monumental Questions: Would this tribulation end? Would my reading matter (Jonathan Franzen's *The Corrections*) inform our particular flavor of dysfunction? Was there a way to uninternalize being a disappointment?

Why did Mother prefer Margie over me? Why, further, did Mother opt to lose her muscle tone? There were so very many questions to record and mull over and discuss with my journal. I wondered, should I give it a name? And the odd thing was, no one noticed. Wherever I landed in the Stout household, my cheap little stick-pen moved constantly across the pages, racing toward engagement.

This sometimes made me sick. Shouldn't I make more effort to engage with *real* people, *reality* itself? But all efforts led invariably to the Dark Ho-hum into which Mother fell sleeping or the Father fled in his aged, crooked way down to his own dim cavern in the basement to fiddle with his nostalgia. They simply fled connection. I realized, in this context, how much my own flight west over thirty years earlier made sense. Dwarfed by the bold landscape, by the wind-chiseled, active volcanoes, I might be a speck, but at least I was a dot in the drama, and not a bit of drab in the dark belly of Ho-hum.

My journal might as well have been a sentient being. It alone expressed curiosity about my experience, agreeing that it was, indeed, bizarre and lonely here. My hand could not drop the pen and do something normal, like scratch or help with dinner, but needed instead to stay attached, racing over the wide-lined, white pages of the second grade–style notebook, with its marbled cover. And although no one noticed, I suspected people knew that the Stout daughter was not normal. Lillian, their cleaning lady of forever, might express a happiness to see me, glad of a witness to "all I am doing for them." On I'd write, while wafting sympathy her way. And however eagerly I awaited any member of the hospice team who might appear and talk with me, I retained a self as moving pen, working its observations across the page.

Over time, instead of observing and recording what I saw, I was observing myself observing and recording what I saw, and the whole thing began to feel insane. Since no one—not parents, not nurses, not visiting friends—asked me what I thought about the Mother Situation, my journal gestured from its corner and asked eagerly, *What's* really *going on?* or, *Get a load of Shirley—is she nuts saying that stuff to your mother?* or, *Your mother, for heaven's sake—what in the world is keeping her alive? Surely it's not that she hasn't yet had her fill of bad TV and undigested Christian Science.*

So, whenever I returned from Bethlehempennsylvania, I was mad to make actual, exterior connection—hence, the urgency to "get a job." Plus, when Mother called again, which might happen any minute, even though I'd been back for only a day, I'd be able to say, "I can't come. I can't take time off *work*, Mom. There is my job!" This would convince her; this would be the truth, although to an outside ear, privileging a job, say, in the deli department of my local grocery store over the wishes of a Dying Parent could sound only cold and abnormal.

But, in truth, there nagged my age-old yearning to be part of a team. This predated even my morgue fantasy. Obviously, the team thing was a result of my having grown up an only child, an *adopted* only child. Like little boys who know deep down that they are truly little girls, and vice versa, I knew that somewhere deep inside me was the belief that I was, at core, a middle-middle child in a family of seventeen. I reasoned that the adult version of my inner middle-middle child was a fixation on Team Membership.

When I shared this fantasy with friends, they would ask, "What exactly do you mean, 'team'?" And I couldn't say, really.

Which, of course, was embarrassing, as all I came up with was, "Well, it entails a white coat. I would be a part of my team by virtue of my white coat."

"Like, a lab coat, maybe?" reasonably, they'd ask, which brought to mind doctors, and going on rounds with other white lab coats, to which I added the images of soft-soled shoes and clipboards. But I worried that membership on a team like this required further education. I mean, at a certain point there is such a thing as *enough*. I do not mean enough learning or broadening or evolving. I mean enough going to school with the intent of feeling finally grown up if you just major in the right thing. At some point (i.e., fifty-plus), this becomes pathetic. So, of course, it made me nervous that part of being a team required more schooling, of a highly specialized and terribly expensive nature, because I kept imagining that this collegial fantasy landed me in the middle of a flock of neurological surgeons. Now, I don't know a lot about this field, but I'm positive it would put me in school for the rest of my life, and then I'd be dead before I even got fitted for my lab coat. I ascertained that I needed to refine my definition of the team.

I found an empty table on the patio above Larry's. Trish was not in evidence. I pulled out my pen and journal. Writing in such a public place offered a salubrious antidote to the truth that in my parents' home, I remained largely unseen. Here, passersby smiled and waved at me like Team Members.

While I waited for thought and wondered how to find a job, the most amazing thing happened: Richard Chamberlain walked by. Since a Sandra Bullock thrill of six months earlier, Belltown had been sadly bereft of celebrity sightings. And here, dangling a small white sack, lips pursed in a silent whistle, was Richard Chamberlain walking right by me. Immediately I began to hum "Edelweiss." This was not random. He was appearing at the Seattle Rep in a production of *The Sound of Music*. I had seen the posters. My heart went *thump*; it leapt; it flattened itself like flung putty; it picked itself up from my chest floor and sighed in a manner reminiscent of cartoon ardor. Dr. Kildair, you see, had been the first object toward which I aimed my sexual budding. I would have known Richard Chamberlain anywhere, even though the man who walked by, dangling his little bit of takeout, was in his sixties, with thin, submissive hair.

I was paralyzed by the shock of recognition, the jolt of witnessing a cultural icon idle by. I did not want his autograph, no surrogate for such feelings. I don't believe in collecting autographs. I go out of my way *not* to collect them. I will stand in line at a book signing, book in hand, and when I arrive at the author's table, I compliment him or her and then whip out a book by a completely different author and ask the author to sign that. This amuses me greatly. I have an original edition of Gretel Ehrlich's *The Solace of Open Spaces* autographed by Rosellen Brown.

But before I could think of what to say or do, he shut down his face, made his features flat as a cracker, and repursed his lips, blowing out a little air, a soupçon of a whistle.

WITH MOTHER'S ENDLESS DYING, I OCCUPIED A DULL zone, pricked by dread. Any minute, there would be another Pennsylvania visit in which nothing happened and less changed, for by the time I would arrive, all clarity about Mother's condition would have vanished, and once again, in the Parents' mind, I would have come not to help negotiate the Significant

Event but to cook her breakfast egg—four minutes and twenty seconds—or help her onto the potty or flatter her that she was looking well.

I returned each time armed with pens and notebook. My observations, if not precious and acute, saved me from sinking beside Mother into Eternal Sloth. I forced my eyes to celebrate light and color, my ears to tease melody from the chords of heavy silence, to breathe in sync with Mother's oxygen machine. How long would it go on—the verbal and emotional non sequiturs, the unintended hurts, the stalwart denial of emotions, the piles of vapid Christian Science? I cannot ask you to go back with me on all those visits. I feel you must know by now the Household Silence, the Obese Margie Miasma, the ritual crab cake dinners, my ill-shod treks around the dead and rusted behemoth of Bethlehem Steel, the hope for contact and connection, and its perpetual dash. What more need you know?

This is how my final trips will be remembered.

I TEND TO MY MOTHER'S NEEDS—HELPING HER TO THE potty, feeding, fetching. Her shoulders rise and fall with the effort of her coughing. The back of her hair is perfectly flat. More precisely, there is no hair on the back of her head, because she lies in bed day and night, and her hair has rubbed away, and what's left is pushed wildly out to the sides. Two coarsely woven fans adorning the sides of her face, this hair is more visually arresting than horrific. I follow Mother as she toddles on her walker from the dining room table back to bed and focus on the flat back of her head, the darling wing shapes, the bony shoulders that her fragile weight pushes up through her mother's white cardigan.

When she says, at bedtime, "Oh, I want to dance with you, and eat ice cream, and listen to music. I want these things so badly," what can I say? No Buddhist lines or aphorisms spring to mind, no placating clichés. Just "May I take your glasses off for sleep? Shall I turn out the light?" Then she nods sweetly, not clinging to the passionately voiced desire of a moment ago, indicating some truth ascertained by the Buddhists—that the mind slides from want to whim, from whim to want, and round again. She is a thought parade, propped between bony shoulders.

In the garden, I weed out the stinging nettles. A lawn mower chokes and roars. Occasionally, Lillian's yellow rubber gloves flash into my line of vision like the beak of an exotic bird. I deadhead the leggy purple pansies, collapsed upon themselves. I weed and water. There is invasive growth afoot between the clusters of impatiens. It used to be I'd sneer at the parched earth and uninspired plantings in my parents' fallow garden, but now I stretch out my tasks until there's nothing left to do. The plants are so deliberately low maintenance as to invite abuse. I study the yellow pansies floating amid the purple ones; the three parched hostas; a diminutive bleeding heart. It's good to bring the living things back from neglect. I engage them lovingly, poking air into the soil, misting them from the ancient hose. It's as if I am responding to their response; the plants are the only things responding to my ministrations. With water, the thirsty leaves deepen in color almost instantly. The geranium at the end of the deck makes a furiously crimson flower before my eyes; the impatiens thicken. My parents have never been outdoor people, have never once enjoyed an evening on their deck for cocktails, dinner, fresh air. Their little patch is serviceable, a nod to the conventions of the neighbors. The patch has a thick layer of beauty bark, and the only things that thrive in that medium are ivy and sow bugs and nettles.

Thunderstorms are predicted. The Father is in the basement, soldering wires and tinkering with the innards of things. Momentarily on her own, Mother rests on the potty, trying to move her bowels. I sit on the deck in an old porch chair, its vinyl latticework shredding a bit more with every shift of my bottom, and study the results of my garden tidying. There is a breeze. The air is soft, its movement a reprieve. The pansies stand erect and purple. The sunlight casts everything in a pink glow.

And my parents will make it to their sixty-second wedding anniversary. When asked by Jackie the hospice nurse, "What's your secret?" the Father says, "Always give in," pleased with this bit of gentle humor, and lifts my mother's hands and cradles them in his. His chin trembles. He doesn't stop the trembling, nor does he turn away. He has accepted unflinchingly Mother's every health disaster but hasn't found a way, in the moments of walking her and feeding her and fetching, to address death as a key player.

And the next day, I will write her eulogy. "Just a few sentences," the Father will reassure me. "That shouldn't be hard." It will no longer matter that he fails to understand the broken-hearted complexity of this request. So we open the newspaper and search the obituaries for a template, and he says, pointing to the blank on the church form, under the category Achievements and Interests, "Not much to be said for a housewife." He shrugs. "That will be tough. Most of her accomplishments were for the family."

And since the Stouts cannot be considered a big, robust family—their siblings and cousins dead, estranged, or dropped;

Mother's mother in the grave for fifteen years—I realize that he must mean himself. Maybe me, in the sense that Mother strove to rope us into the family corral—the Father and the errant, erring, sometime Daughter.

MOTHER SMELLS SWEET. EVEN HER EXCRETIONS ARE sweet. She reclines in her rumpled, bony heap. There is nothing horrific or disgusting. Her dying is not a horror. We are blessed, or protected, in this way. She reclines with the green telephone cradled by her ear. Her mouth hangs open. She clings to it with a grip that reminds me of a bird's talons encircling a perch. She is receiving Christian Science council from a practitioner woman whom I do not know. She seems rapt or passed out—which, I'm never sure.

When she's dead, I will miss her sweetness. This puzzles me, as I claim to be a feminist, an advocate of rigorous outdoor adventure, a downhill skier, a lifter of weights, and every cell in my body has eschewed, indeed militantly despised, what Mother has aspired to, this limp goal—to be *a lady*.

What self is left? A fretting set of worries and discomforts that are the focus of Mother's attention, such as it is. I do not mind. When she dies, so will go her sweetness. For however manipulative and narcissistic Mother is, it is true—everybody says it—she is sweet. This is what they mean—it is not the crown jewel of a polished character; it is a gaze full of yearning; it is the baby bird's upturned, gaping beak; it is her dear trust and astonishing blankness.

I will remember holding out my hands to Mother as she lets go of the arms on her walker, trusting herself, for a moment, to space. Quivering, she reaches for my hands, and one socked foot ventures a few inches onto the carpeted terrain, followed by the other. The back of her head is a frightful buffalo wallow in miniature, the hairs standing straight up. She looks at me, and her eyes are pools of *where?* and *can I?* She wobbles toward the sofa, asking, "Where are we going?" even though a moment ago she stated boldly, "Take me to the sofa."

In these moments, Mother is . . . who? Who is she, this toddler, almost eighty-four? Who is she, this old darling, settled for sleep, the white afghan drawn over her legs, another one, autumn colored, wrapping her feet like a package? She looks brightly out of the pools of her eyes, slaps her heart with her hand, and exclaims, "I love you. Oh, I love you." Who makes this declaration? For whom does she bear such love? Something in me does not want to say good night. Something in me makes me want to linger, in spite of the gaps in her attention, the non sequiturs, the meanness.

Something in me wants to linger, privileged to stroke her brow, and study the bones there, to pat the eyebrows with my thumb. She remains so hungry for touch. She is not my mother, she who lies here. She is not that old sack of limitations, disappointments, yearnings, fear. Who lies here? What in me does not want to say good night?

I know. I know I'm being redundant; I recite these teensy details over and over, as if, in repetition, the sweet and the mean, poignancy and poison will coalesce, purified. As if by putting the details on parade, all the complicated, contradictory layers will be made concrete. Over time, something shifts, each reexamined detail melting the hurts a little more, warming them.

If there were a ceremony called Waiting for Death, it would include mostly the quotidian—we replenish the liquids in her glass; we bathe her and lower her to the potty and wait with her while she empties her bladder and bowel; we keep watch. With a slight flourish, I drape the afghan over legs and feet. Turn the flowers sent from Hilma, Jeanne, or Nan so that she might see them at their best angle and, when she doesn't care, not plummet into blame and disappointment. The bitter grip of disappointment eases. With that comes peace.

And so, finally, I ceased to suffer my parents' household as if fighting for my life. It was just a dying woman, whittled down to seventy-two pounds; it was just an old man, functioning as well as he could with his angry joints and grief. It was just a forever-fifty-year-old woman, writing in a wing chair on a brilliant morning in late summer. For the first in the many times I was called back, this time, I would be loath to leave.

And so now I'll cut to the chase. Six months after the April visit, Mother was moved from the house to a hospice facility. Imagining my life my own again, free of guilt and importuning, I rejoiced in the imminent end.

EIGHTEEN

⇋

Blue Toes, Silver Ashes

BELIEVING THE MODEST, ELEVEN-BED HOSPICE FACILITY to be a luxury hotel located in the memory of her many trips to Switzerland, Mother exhorted the Father, every day, to "tip the staff." Occasional puffs of lucidity pierced these charmed delusions, as when, for example, she vowed not to leave the building by the "back door." She recognized that to be the way out for the corpses.

Every day my father and I visited. The thick heat of summer had loitered into fall. I wore shorts and a T-shirt from morning until bedtime. Mother, as she drifted in and out of sleep or floated on the currents of dementia, never tired of sharing her disapproval of my outfit. Indeed, hyperaware of the institution of our Wardrobe Wars, I felt as if, in some perverse way, in the place of better judgment, I had chosen to pack the most tattered pair of shorts, a shred of a faded T-shirt, and dissolute sandals.

Nevertheless, I determined to ignore Mother's disapproving

gaze and muttering and to fashion myself into something useful. Although it had no prior experience with end-time tasks, my tidy and well-organized mind dwelt on lists—call friends and relatives; review the will; construct the memorial announcement and the official obituary; sort stuff; choose the music, the menu, the memorial bouquet. All of it was on-the-job learning, initially daunting but, in the execution, child's play to a mind unmoved by grief.

IN THE LITANY OF DAYS LEADING TO HER LAST DAY, I remember only moments. I forced myself to meet the undertaker, fearing a ghoulish and Dickensian encounter. Like Reverend Quail's, his too, was a bird name, Heron. A round and earthy man, John Heron greeted me in a blindingly white shirt with French cuffs. His purely white hair framed his pink face, and he looked, therefore, like a valentine. A cigar smoldered in the ashtray. He addressed me as the one in charge, which was fine, because I was. My first duty in this capacity was to inform the Father that some cemetery fee had leaped from $90 to $400, and that this was not the undertaker's fault.

The days flowed and pooled against one another. On Sunday mornings, the Father wound his clocks. These faithful rounds reminded me of how tenaciously he fed Mother, how rattled he became when she rejected food. Against her refusal, he'd poke a loaded fork, as if fueling her will to live. His hope fastened on every bite negotiated. The Father was not attuned to her body—the mouth that dutifully received; the mouth that made a stab at mastication; the little heart heaving in its prison; the face staring up, obeying his need for her to chew, swallow, live. There was a war inside my mother, her body a sagging heap of skin and fragile tissue. Something in her wanted to quit, but "She eats!" everyone exclaimed, and when they did, she beamed back like a little girl, all dressed up and beautifully performing. She eats. There is applause.

Her heart thrashed inside her. How long could it possibly survive its furious gait? One day, Mother spiked a fever. "Normal," the nurse said, and left the room. The Father and I looked at each other. The question hung, unasked: Normal for what? Was it a precursor? This particular nurse had a gift for mumbled innuendo. She'd deliver crucial information with postural and facial reassurance, and so one felt manipulated into believing there had been an actual exchange, when, in fact, the substance was elliptical.

"I'll go ask her what she meant, " I said, and briskly left the room.

I found an articulate nurse in the kitchen and asked her. Fever was, indeed, another milestone in the Journey of Decline. The brain was exhausted and unable to regulate the body's temperature. The brain was saying, *Enough*. It was the body shutting down.

"She's not going to wake up," the Father said, after I explained about "normal." I hoped he meant that it was time to go home for the night, and not that she'd never look at him again. He bent stiffly and kissed her forehead. "Good night, darling," every part of him said, and then he shuffled toward the door. I bent to kiss Mother's clammy forehead, putting the salt of her fever on my lips. Guiltily, I wondered if, like a cold, I'd catch her dying. I tasted her. She was on my lips—her salt, her battle. Furtively, I patted my lips with a napkin.

"Good night" was still "good night" and not "good-bye."

⇌

WHEN HER HEART RATE ELEVATED TO AN ALARMING 168, Theresa, the night nurse, advised sedating Mother. The struggles that appeared to ravage her shrunken body surely indicated, in the nurse's estimation, some psychological stress, and Theresa couldn't believe it when Mother smiled sweetly and refused. Her legs and feet twitched in response to her thudding heart. "What keeps you here, Elizabeth?" she asked gently.

Mother, eyes shining, cried out, "Life!"

And then a thought rolled through her. She turned her head and looked at me full on.

"Are you glad I am your mummie?" she asked.

I looked at her stupidly, drawing a blank.

Theresa and the Father stared at me from the foot of her bed. It was like I'd forgotten my lines on opening night. I looked at them as if for my cue. *Oh, just say it to her*, I addressed my heart, trying to wring warmth from impatience. The size of Mother's need crashed against the gist of my experience as her child. I could not say it.

"Say it," she said fiercely. "Say, 'I am so glad you are my mummie.'"

I couldn't—could not ooze one small plop of gratitude. I squeezed her hand, hoping this would do. It did not. She said again, looking at me with a combination of ferocity and sweetness—"Say it"—and, mimicking her singsong voice, but with no conviction, I repeated, "I am so glad." History's weight and truth's ropy complications pressed on my vocal apparatus, making it more natural to gag.

"What?" she asked, her eyes bright and innocent. She was

egging me on, I knew, although of course Theresa and the Father thought it all so poignant, all so end-time sweet.

"What?" I repeated, my eyes a parody of hers.

"Say again, 'I am so glad that you are my mummie.'"

Again I looked to them, as if they would throw me my forgotten line from the wings. "She wants you to say it back," Theresa said helpfully, with a darling twinkle, so free of history's curse.

There was nothing to do but say it. "I am so glad you are my mummie," I said. There was a "goddamn it" tone to the delivery.

I wanted her dead. It was that simple.

ONE MORNING, THE FATHER WAS CLAWING THROUGH memories in the basement when the phone rang.

"It was the nurse," he said, pulling himself up the stairs. "She says Elizabeth has begun to show signs of active dying." His words were broken by sobs, and I reached out to hold him.

Naturally, when we got there, she wasn't. I resigned myself, knowing this would be, if not the Day, a Waiting Day, full of dull amusements—mediocre food, bad coffee, walks between bedside and parking lot, bedside and parking lot. I would sit between the hot metal of shiny cars in my stocking feet, relishing the fact that those who came and went would not find this odd. Death had relaxed our habits, wardrobes, and routines. There was something exceedingly poignant about dwelling in death's presence. Strict observance of a day's routines compared poorly to the imprecation to seize on what was precious.

For a while, I sat by the bed, petting her emaciated form,

holding her bird-claw hands, marveling at the veins in her neck, at her mouth pulling wretchedly at the air. The window was open above her bed. Birdsong drifted in. An autumnal crispness began to pierce the malingering summer. Her mother had also died in late October.

"It won't be long now," the hospice nurses said, always sweetly, the words "long" and "now" still without measure.

WHEN IT BEGAN TO SEEM THAT SHE COULDN'T POSSIBLY last much longer, I asked the Father, "Have you had the Talk?" He looked at me with his bright eyes, chin trembling, and shook his head no.

"It might be time for you to have your . . . private talk," I said. "I'll leave you to your privacy." For a moment I believed that, because of my suggestion, they would understand it was time to let each other go.

MOTHER'S TOES TURNED BLUE. THE NURSE INFORMED US that it was another one of *those indications*. I sent the Father away to get some lunch, so that Mother and I could have our Talk. "I'll miss you," I said to the agony that was her breathing, to the O of her mouth, to her closed eyes. I wasn't sure what I might be missing, if perhaps just the intensity of these times spent with her—their final cessation. I didn't see the point of trying to say or feel more.

"You had a good little talk," I said. "I hope it was Important. I hope it was the Talk and he told you he could let you go." I could not get over the fact that her toes were blue.

⇋

IN SPITE OF MOTHER'S DETERMINATION NOT TO DIE, IN spite of her vow that she would never leave through the back door, she had to make her exit. I was not there when Mother died. That didn't surprise me. I regarded the moment of her dying as one of profound leave-taking between my parents, and it was not mine to share. At 10:10 on a Wednesday night, in late October, as I was cleaning up my dinner dishes, I got a call from the nurse saying that Mother had died.

I entered the room on tiptoe. My father sat holding his dead wife's hand. Before Mother's, I had never seen or touched a corpse, never been in death's presence. That was the idiom I bore in mind—"the presence of death"—as if I'd found myself in the room with the pope or a police sergeant, some formidable character who was going to make me think I should at least take off my hat.

I knew death first by her body's stillness—no more galloping heart, no more hiss of the oxygen machine. I stroked her hair and cheeks, noting that she was still warm. Her mouth was somewhat open, frozen, but not in an expression of surprise. Her forehead was smooth. Her arms lay limp at her sides. She was neither stiff nor cold, and so she wasn't gone entirely. She was still Mother. I wasn't ready to have her be a corpse. Her body, sweet in illness, was also sweet in death. She had worn nothing but a nightie for half a year—that and her mother's white cardigan and an assortment of fuzzy socks. I lifted the covers. Her feet were bare. Her toes were pink again. I arranged the thin blanket over her feet, as if protecting her from the next phase of her journey, which would be the morgue. I looked at my father, wondering if I needed his permission to stroke and pet her. She belonged to me, too, I thought defensively, but he was too exhausted to feed our old rivalry.

I unstrapped her watchband, noting the thin white streaks of salt on the inside of the band, where her sweat had made patterns. I lifted her hand, still pliant, still warm, twisting the ring off her finger. I spoke to her as I tugged it off, promising to put it in a safe place, to keep our connection through her wedding ring. And this was my moment of Unfettered Care, this removal of the ring, this gesture fueled by tenderness. In this moment, my mother couldn't defend against my love.

I had become so familiar with her body that it was impossible to believe that the next contact would be with ashes. There was no gradual progression from Warm Corpse to Ashes. John Heron had asked, thoughtfully, if he could box me up "a child's portion" after the cremation. Honestly, that's what he'd said. And then would come the grave. There had to be more and better gestures easing the transition from Warm Corpse to Ashes—more stroking and patting; bathing and dressing; adjusting to the permanence of this good-bye. Bereft of a good transition, my heart was restless and unsatisfied. I yearned to go with her to the morgue, to lift her onto the cold slab, to stand by when they slid her into the cooler. It wasn't right to send her on her way alone with strangers. I should ride with her to the funeral home; I should dress her before cremation. I should watch as she was rolled into the crematorium and, afterward, study the ashes for identifying fragments. Do not think me ghoulish. I am only embodied substance trying to understand the journey of our flesh.

As it is, we would stand at the graveside on an exquisitely clear, blue-sky day, on an October morning, finally and appropriately crisp. There would have been an acknowledgment of Mother's passing only by virtue of a change in our routine. Our flesh, baffled, would feel cheated.

ON THE MORNING OF MOTHER'S LITTLE SERVICE FOR THE two of us, John Heron picked us up, officious and scrubbed, still the pinkest man I had ever seen. He offered his condolences and then asked when he should present the bill. We drove to the cemetery in his dove-gray hearse, enveloped in thick leather and plumes of cigar. We were confronted with an awning and a hole. Fallen leaves blew and rustled. The drone of maintenance machines and staccato voices of the crew broke the stillness. Squirrels tore through the leaves. John Heron guided my father's elbow to the hole underneath the awning. Four folding chairs had been placed before the hole, two padded, two not. The undertaker's daughter shuffled them so that ours would be padded.

We wore wool coats. The Father was flanked by the birdmen. Reverend Quail, with his curiously parted hair, began to lead himself in prayer, requesting that God grant His beloved Elizabeth her rest, blah, blah. John Heron asked if he should place the ashes in the hole. But the Father should. This seemed clear. He should be the one to place her ashes in the grave that they would share, and I should be keeping my hand upon his shoulder, present but at a courteous remove, as I held my child's portion of my mother's ashes.

I said to John Heron, "Let him do it. Do you want to do it, Pop?"

With a quiver, he nodded, and then Heron and Quail rushed to his side to anchor the Father's armpits as he lowered himself stiffly with the urn. He planted Mother's ashes in the round hole. They were in a box the size of a Whitman's Sampler. All that history, all those bones, hair of my mother, teeth and eyes of my mother, repinked toes—all had been reduced to the size of a two-pound box of chocolates.

They raised him up. It took a while, as he was shaking. We stood for a moment, and then he looked at John Heron, his eyes watery behind huge glasses, and asked, "Is my hole here, too, or behind her?"

Heron blinked, uncomprehending.

"For me," he continued. "For when I'm here."

I looked at Heron. "Would it be possible for my father to go beside her, in the same hole?" I asked, translating. I looked at the fragile little man, my father. "Would you like that, Pop?" I asked.

He nodded. "Yes," he said, as if a troubling detail of the itinerary in a complicated journey had been settled.

"It can be arranged," John Heron said.

"There is certainly enough room for two," I said.

The Father turned to me abruptly, pivoting with the force of a new idea. "There is certainly enough room for *three*," he said. "You can have a place here with us, if you want it."

I thanked him, pretending to ponder this curious invitation as, mentally, I began to pack for home.

⇌

Commentary:

OVER TIME

THE FEELINGS I DESCRIBED REPRESENTED, ULTIMATELY, my liberation from pain and paralyzing blame and my transition to a purer form of love and tenderness for Mother, freed of disappointment. In that respect, there were no lies in what I wrote.

It being evening, I would have, if home, begun to make my dinner, accompanied by a lovely glass of wine. Since this wasn't home, I had to scrounge for food and drink. Pop's idea of a suitable larder consisted of tiny amounts of astonishingly dull foods—saltines; frozen peas; "fresh" carrots gone limp; margarine; bread that only hinted at the staff of life; skim milk and Wheaties; a handful of fruits, out of season; and always Postum. The liquor larder offered even less. I'd go down to the cluttered basement and explore the options, systematically depleted by my visits over the past two years. I'd rattle around the cupboard for what remained. Obviously, it had not been restocked. I took sad inventory—a dusty bottle of generic Scotch; a half-full, heart-shaped bottle of Armagnac; terrible New York state wine; a little sherry; grenadine. All awful, awful. The collection absolutely lacked anything reminiscent of a well-coordinated and committed bar. This last trip, it would be Scotch.

Up came the bottle. Out of the fridge came the broccoli I'd purchased earlier, from the cupboard a tube of pasta.

Nothing complicated. Set a pretty table; riffle through Pop's video collection for a movie; manufacture some dessert.

The movie was *Out of Africa*. I drank and felt better, even though I no longer cared for Scotch. My receded self, she who served by day, prohibited from expressing her true nature, plumped like a sliver of dry sponge in water. Music could be heard again; windows were thrown open. Slipping into the cocoon of alcohol, I could retrieve the amputated bits of my authenticity and greet them. I was exhausted.

I don't remember the words used to inform me that it was over, when I answered the phone. One of the nurses had offered to come and get me. I drank a glass of water, brushed my teeth, hoping to cover whatever fumes lingered from Scotch. This moment had seemed to come over and over, and I had ceased distinguishing between the fact of it and fantasy. I thought, naively, now that she had finally died, now that I was done, I could leave instantly, board a plane tonight, tomorrow. So when, a little later, the Father said I'd have to stay for five more days, could leave only after the memorial service that seemed to be mine to plan, the truly unendurable descended.

It had been cold comfort that the sum of my experience with Mother had been, as I thought, duty in the absence of love. Now I see it differently. I would never not have obeyed her summons to "come home," however reluctantly executed. I thought, then, it was for her, and him, although less so. But something else happened—a process that burned away the old impurities. In performing the end-time tasks, and in bearing witness to the courtship between death and my mother, I felt the narrative shift. Although now my relationship with Mother consists of memory and memories revised and whatever comfort I derive from believing that, for all the imperfections, there was love, there is, in addition, the relief in having no regrets. That is, having made myself available to duty, I never have to squirm with the remorse of having not shown up.

NINETEEN

⇌

The Shelf Life of Ashes

I DID NOT KNOW WHERE TO PUT WHAT OF MOTHER I brought home. The idea of carrying her in ash form seemed just plain funny. Tucked inside a Ziploc sandwich bag, in turn stuffed into a plastic so-called "urn," she weighed in at a couple of ounces.

Perhaps this has happened to you: the prickly parent is finally dead. You wait for grief, imagining its rush in the poignant beholding of the Parent Ashes. With this contact, grief will surely come. You look forward to finding a special urn, symbolically apt, to contain your child's portion. What a small hope, that the Parent Ashes will instigate a flicker of the memory of warmth between you. But the container remains inert—a pure, white, plastic, columnar shape. It says nothing. You ponder the oddity of holding the bone and teeth bits of your parent. That is what was left, and I kept feeling nothing.

I had a cat named Adam, whom I loved. He was a courtly cat—tabby, in part, with a white chest and paws. When Adam was hit by a car and killed, I felt relief that the waiting was over. No longer would I have to live with the daily dread of loss. It had happened, and my unencumbered affection was no longer susceptible to dread and worry. Although surprised by this thought, I was also proud, as it indicated that I could manage grief, could think myself through it, had bypassed the awful, endless night of it.

A friend carried his body, still perfectly intact, into the carport and laid him on a bench. I smiled, feeling calm and peaceful. My gaze lingered, noting the perfect curve of wrist and delicacy of paw. I said out loud, "I'll never touch his paws again." And then started crying.

I wrapped Adam in a bolt of unbleached muslin. I cut long, rough sprigs of rosemary, as if to dress and anoint his body before burial. I looked at my friends through a teary blur. I said, "It looks as if we're going to roast him."

Alex, my former Lopez Island love, and I drove two hours north to Gold Bar, the place where I got him, and buried him in the meadow. Mt. Index declared itself in the near distance. Then we walked up to the adjoining state park called Wallace Falls. We followed the trail all the way up to where it ended and began clambering up the boulders. They were slick with the spray of the crashing falls. The water roared over the edge at a sickening pitch and dropped a hundred feet. A tree had snagged on the boulders halfway down. It jutted out, resembling, horribly, a human limb trapped there. The pull of the roaring falls, the plunge so easily imagined, the devilish chill— all of it was the analogue to grief.

Mother's ashes held no key to grief. I put them here; I put them there, moving the urn restlessly from place to place—a drawer, a shelf, a table, a windowsill. I was afraid that if I didn't keep touching and moving the "urn," I'd forget it and lose her forever. I thought about taking the ashes out into nature, as I had Adam's body, and opening the container to let her drift on the wind. But Mother had no affinity for the beautiful, wild mountains, nor had she ever trusted nature.

The metaphor conjured by her ashes moved me more than her death: all that had come of my seeking to know my mother and yearning to be known by her was contained in a tiny bag of ashes.

Would I miss my mother? I don't think so. Maybe when someone for whom you bear a wounded and complicated love takes forever to die, you do the grieving then, an incremental process. Am I mean not to miss her—mean, like holding a grudge, like we're little girls and she has called me something nasty, and so every time we pass each other in the hall, I take another opportunity to snub her? Or like I'm more focused on putting something disgusting in her sandwich in the lunch-room than I am on trying to discover a common taste that we might share?

In an ideal realm, end time brings gentling qualities to smooth the past, like a blanket of fresh snow. Disappointments soften; grievances turn into a recognition of gifts; differences in style and manner are less cause for rage and horror. A kind of distillation happens in this ideal realm—the old, dark, rough-edged stuff gets burned up, and the ash of sweetness settles. Mother and I might have looked at each other from a kinder place and known that we were in the soup together. That's the journey I wanted to make with her, a release from the grip of history's fears and disappointments. Such a release might point one toward the Map of Aging Well.

⇌

HAS THE QUEST FAILED—OR HAVE I FAILED THE QUES-
tion? In the end, has this been a book about failure? In
revisiting the manuscript years after its first "completion," did
I not intend to address this? The quest—to find the Map of
Aging Well—failed. It was bound to. Consider whom I studied.

And what did I finally do with Mother's ashes? For years,
I moved them from place to place, believing that some *place*,
the right place, would honor her pebbly remains. Frustrated, I
thought it might be that I hadn't found a beautiful container,
and so I shopped but continued to find nothing, and she
remained for five years in her small baggie, which in turn
remained in the white plastic box, my child's portion.

I began to notice that I kept calling her ashes "she," as in,
"She's over there, by the toaster" or, "She'd like to hear something this morning on the classical station on the radio." I
found myself wanting "her" to talk to me, to bring words of
comfort from beyond, or even just to reminisce a little.

I moved them into my bedroom, on the windowsill, by the
window seat. There she might admire the garden. But then I'd
move them back to my study, on the shelf beside the bronze
Buddha, and for years I moved them in this way, and of course
I'd forget where, and then I would come upon them and the
whole mystery of where they should reside begin again.

One night, as I walked out of my neighborhood bookstore,
across the patio of the Cuban café, El Diablo, I experienced
my aging as a sensation. I observed vibrant clusters of the Young
—couples bending toward each other, their ideas sensuously
entwined; singles propped before novels and laptops. I passed
this café, filled to the brim with discussion and keyboard

tapping and the buzz of opinion building and celebration—a hive of thoughts rubbing against thoughts. Thrilling, this cross-pollination of ideas, like sex in the air—all that possibility, the unknown, a mystery still with friendly overtones. Not that I was envious, only aware that I was no longer new. It wasn't feeling old so much as feeling no longer new.

Mother died. The Father teetered toward her. He was valiant. He was carrying on. In his engineer's way, the systems and routines of his life granted him, then, a final share of meaning. And I am trying to end this book. I am not old like "my" old people. I am in the middle. I am not old; that is, I am not diminished, fragile, holding the imminence of my death in mind like fruit in a sack. I am not young; that is, I am not *pleine d'omnipotence* and ever high on the drug of endless possibility.

FIVE YEARS PASSED, AND AT SOME POINT I WON A $300 gift certificate to a garden nursery, whose specialty was native plants. I made the trip in early spring—it was a drizzly, chilly day in a particularly drizzly, chilly pocket of the Pacific Northwest. I slogged through a vast tumble of as-yet-unleafed, unruly shrubs and chaotic rows of young conifers. Banks of ferns and fringe-cup flowers proliferated underneath the hemlocks. It put me in the mind of a visit to an old auto graveyard, grown over with grass, somewhat depressing with all the tumble and divots and spill. The weather enhanced my misery. I chose cartfuls of plants, my greed piqued and satisfied, but soon a soft voice of panic and sharp regret arose, as now or as soon as possible I'd have to actually site and plant my acquisitions.

Returning home, I didn't plant immediately. I walked around the garden over the next few days, trying to make good choices about siting the twenty-seven native bleeding hearts, the forty ferns, the seventeen starts of fringe-cup flower. And then I came across a broken egg, the blue of a robin's egg. I remembered one of my favorite gifts I'd given Mother, a necklace consisting of a graceful silver armature, in its curve resting a pale, smooth, oval turquoise, this robin's-egg blue. When she opened the package, she gasped, lifting it out. "This is the most beautiful gift I have ever gotten," she said, and it pierced my heart.

I stooped and gathered the bits of shell. Then I thought of Mother's ashes, and of the twenty-seven native bleeding hearts. And that was how I came to "bury" Mother—under a small, hand-mounded berm, planted with bleeding hearts, a miniature dry creek bed of pebbles wending over and through it, and the scattered bits of blue shell.

How did I feel about putting Mother's ashes underneath a drift of bleeding hearts? I'd like to say that it was perfect, for I had carried this troubling bundle from room to room, shelf to sill, for five years, and I think in the end I was simply relieved to have found some place for them—out of sight, finally, and maybe out of mind.

Upon shaking out the contents of the plastic urn, I invited Large Feeling. None came. I truly tried to enter each moment like a diver, feeling the intensity of the water—its resistance, its gradient cool, its many shades of vegetal green. I truly tried to greet the cool, tiny mound of earth, the surrounding plantings—daphne, cranesbill, jasmine, *Alchemilla mollis*, all fine-sounding names. I had expected an accompanying feeling of resolve, a sigh of closure. Both eluded me, and really, what is closure? The hope for a pain or a terrible mystery to resolve. A hope only. Dreams will carry the pain and the mystery, embedding them in mood and tissue.

I had wanted the ashes to nudge me into recognizing my own future of ash. I tipped the contents to sift through my fingers. It could have been charred residue from the fireplace. It was just crumbled bits of incinerated bone. Nothing of her remained. Just the reminder, so easily ignored, that this substance will be me someday; that this substance, once my mother, was now just a drifting, dusty medium that could, as I opened the baggie, either waft up on the breeze or lend texture to the bit of loamy earth it was consigned to.

THIS HAS BEEN A BOOK ABOUT FAILURE. HOW IN THE world could I have expected grace and resolution from such insubstantial models, feeding on their thin gruel of fear, bitterness, and disappointment? But perhaps you've known this all along and predicted that my fear of aging and dying would actually intensify. I concluded from Mother's fierce refusal to die—to actually outlive her doctors' prognosis by two full years—that death is dreadful. Before its grip, she felt herself an infant dangled over a craggy abyss, at the bottom of which rushed icy mountain torrents.

I will remember that Mother died, finally, in late October, and that it had stayed unusually warm. The air had changed only slightly. It was no longer sultry but not yet crisp. I will remember the walk I had to take every single day of every visit to keep hold of myself—through the cemetery, down the ancient lane, buckled and broken by tree roots. *Only look up*, I would remind myself. *Only look up*, because my thoughts were heavy, and the path was so uneven, and when I remembered to look up, there, welcoming, would be the long corridor of stately sycamores with perfect crowns, a hundred feet tall, their mottled bark like the skin of savanna mammals, their boughs thick and strong. The seedpods of the sycamores and their spatulate leaves covered the ground over which they towered. They represented the beauty of shape and symmetry and how things are, which is to say, messy in their perfection.

I will remember myself as trying too hard and failing to connect with my experience, or so I thought. The trees welcomed my walking and softened my judgment. They seemed to let me off the hook, saying I did not have to be good in the face of Mother's dying, only present, just a woman trying too hard, wearing sneakers with red laces, out on her daily walk through the cemetery where her mother soon would lie.

ACKNOWLEDGMENTS

I am grateful to the literary journal, *Prairie Schooner*, which published an excerpt of the memoir, "The Perfidy of Things," and to the support of various institutions which encouraged my work along the way, among which were: Hedgebrook, for a wondrous writing residency, and the Ludwig Vogelstein Foundation, for a generous grant.

Without the acceptance and guidance of She Writes Press, and the collaborative input, appreciative humor, perspicacity and skill of my editor, Annie Tucker, this memoir would have moldered in a box.

Teachers along the way, although not explicitly connected with the work, nevertheless helped me, as a practitioner and a writer, to cultivate a kinder, more inquiring mind, and so I toast Ruth Denison and Julie Wester.

I would like to also thank those friends and family members who have exuded a warm and steady confidence in this book—that it was worthy, and that it will succeed. Thanks to Dana and the kids—Lily and Susannah Ellis—and their terrific mates, Dave and Devin, and the dozen or so readers who gave their time early in the book's development, who urged me on. And thanks, of course, to Harriet.

Finally, I must give thanks to my parents, now dead, who provided the means for the many anguished, albeit fertile trips back and forth to *where it all began*, and the subsequent surfeit of material.

May all beings be happy.
May all beings be free of suffering.

ABOUT THE AUTHOR

photo credit: Sonnet Lauberth

Following her *conventional* education (a BA in Fine Arts with a minor in theater; an MA in English), Hollis Giammatteo moved to Philadelphia where, with a college chum, she founded, managed, and wrote plays for The Wilma Theater. It is thriving, still. She moved west in '79, hungry in that conventional way for all it promised—big nature: mountains, sea and sky—and has called Seattle home since then. Her education, albeit *unconventional*, continued with a playwright-in-residency for the Rhode Island Feminist theater, followed by a cross-country, women's peace walk, On The Line, which she wrote about in a memoir, *On The Line: Memoir of a Peace Walk* (1988). The cultivation of Buddhist meditation practice was the treasure found in those experiences.

Her work has appeared in various magazines and literary journals: *Prairie Schooner, The North American Review, Ms., Calyx, Vogue, Women's Sports and Fitness,* among others. Her awards include a National Endowment for the Arts Literary Fellowship, a residency at the Cottages at Hedgebrook on Whidbey Island, WA, a PEN/Jerard Award, honoring, "a distinguished nonfiction work-in-progress for an emerging woman writer" for *On the Line*. She continues striving to emerge. *The Shelf Life of Ashes* will be her first published memoir.

SELECTED TITLES FROM SHE WRITES PRESS

She Writes Press is an independent publishing company
founded to serve women writers everywhere.
Visit us at www.shewritespress.com.

*Renewable: One Woman's Search for Simplicity, Faithfulness, and
Hope* by Eileen Flanagan. $16.95, 978-1-63152-968-9. At age
forty-nine, Eileen Flanagan had an aching feeling that she wasn't
living up to her youthful ideals or potential, so she started trying
to change the world—and in doing so, she found the courage to
change her life.

From Sun to Sun: A Hospice Nurse's Reflection on the Art of Dying by
Nina Angela McKissock. $16.95, 978-1-63152-808-8. Weary from
the fear people have of talking about the process of dying and
death, a highly experienced registered nurse takes the reader into
the world of twenty-one of her beloved patients as they prepare to
leave this earth.

*Flip-Flops After Fifty: And Other Thoughts on Aging I Remembered
to Write Down* by Cindy Eastman. $16.95, 978-1-938314-68-1. A
collection of frank and funny essays about turning fifty—and all
the emotional ups and downs that come with it.

Learning to Eat Along the Way by Margaret Bendet. $16.95,
978-1-63152-997-9. After interviewing an Indian holy man,
newspaper reporter Margaret Bendet follows him in pursuit of
enlightenment and ends up facing demons that were inside her all
along.

Don't Leave Yet: How My Mother's Alzheimer's Opened My
Heart by Constance Hanstedt. $16.95, 978-1-63152-952-8. The
chronicle of Hanstedt's journey toward independence, self-
assurance, and connectedness as she cares for her mother, who is
rapidly losing her own identity to the early stage of Alzheimer's.

Gap Year Girl by Marianne Bohr. $16.95, 978-1-63152-820-0.
Thirty-plus years after first backpacking through Europe,
Marianne Bohr and her husband leave their lives behind and take
off on a yearlong quest for adventure.